CW00504841

Finding Joy

How To Live Your Life

With

Presence, Purpose

And Authenticity

"I believe if you face into your fears, the messiness and the darkness, you can find your wisdom, joy and light"

- Kath Wynne-Jones

Finding Joy Within™

DISCLAIMER

Author: Kath Wynne-Jones

Title: Finding Joy Within™

ISBN: 9798425241344

DEDICATION

This book is dedicated to my beautiful daughter, Emma.

And to everyone who is on the journey to living a life

filled with joy!

FOREWORD

I'm Annie Grace, author of the best–selling books This Naked Mind and The Alcohol Experiment. Kath is a member of the 'This Naked Mind' community, and I am so honoured that she asked me to write this foreword. Kath and I both know first–hand how intimidating it can be to evaluate your relationship with alcohol and to face your fears of the unknowns of what is on the other side. I'm so proud of Kath for being so vulnerable and sharing her experiences to help others.

Finding Joy Within™ is a beautiful depiction of the painful and rewarding journey of discovering freedom from alcohol. Kath's story of pain, loss, fear, hope and love is so human, so relatable and provides hope for anyone else struggling with their relationship to alcohol. It's not an easy path, as you're about to discover, but as you'll hear in Kath's raw diary–like account of her year–long journey, it is beyond worth it.

Finding Joy Within™ will surely help you feel like you're not alone and will give you amazing tools to help no matter where you are in your particular journey. It will give you an appreciation for everything that made up your past and will show you how to choose happiness now!

Annie Grace - Author of This Naked Mind

CONTENTS

Finding Joy Within™

INTRODUCTION

I have written this book to share my journey of how I changed my life, from one I was, at best surviving, to one that I love and am grateful for every single day.

Until the age of 43, I had been constantly busy and unknowingly using every form of distraction possible: alcohol, food, work, shopping, keeping mega busy... Only when faced with some life-changing events in 2019, did I truly start to apply in a ritualistic way what I had learnt in the personal development, spiritual and therapeutic worlds over the past ten years. 2019 forced me to stop, be patient and look within.

Much of this book focuses on my relationship with alcohol, because that was the biggest domino for me – the thing that I needed to tackle to start to address every other aspect of my life, including looking after my body, growing spiritually, loving my work and loving my life. Alcohol had been a crutch I had used since being a teenager, to help me cope with life. However, I believe the processes and the rituals I have put in place to live a joyful, sober life are equally as applicable to dealing with other negative behaviours, such as eating and work addiction (both of which are featured in here too...).

Outwardly, throughout my life I appeared to have everything: a beautiful daughter, a beautiful home, amazing family and friends, and a great job. However, come the weekends or any stressful situation, Prosecco had become a definite addition to my 'bestie' list. Whilst things may outwardly have appeared okay, inside my head was a living nightmare! I faced constant anxiety, loneliness, fear, shame, lack of self-respect, negativity and misery. A constant voice in my head told me I wasn't good enough and this was tearing me down every minute of the day.

I wasn't what you would term an 'alcoholic' – from the outside you would probably not have thought that drink was a 'problem' for me. I didn't drink every day, I didn't feel tempted to drink in the mornings (well, not many, other than when I was going on holiday! ☺) and I don't have many mad, drunken tales to tell. The greatest excitement I can share consists of stories of embarrassing photos, dancing on tables, singing in karaoke bars and an occasional loss of memory in the morning.

I know there are many people who genuinely use alcohol in moderation to enhance their life, which is brilliant. Unfortunately, that wasn't me. Once I started I didn't have a stop button – leaving a half–opened bottle of wine wasn't an option for me. I knew I was using alcohol to help me manage my stress, anxiety and loneliness, which is not where I wanted to be. As a life coach, with an interest in resilience, i needed to know that I could handle whatever life threw at me without needing something external to get me through it. This is where I had been for the rest of my adult life.

When I decided to quit drinking, I had no idea what I was about to experience. But following what other sober authors, who have been a huge source of comfort and inspiration to me on my journey, have written, I think what I experienced was pretty typical of the alcohol quit process. I have survived through very grim days where I have white–knuckled getting through the day (and have sometimes been in bed by 7pm!). I've had some sad and uneventful days. But most importantly I've had peaceful and often joyful days! What I do know is, that had I not taken this journey to get the numbing substance out of my body, I might never have experienced the nuances of some of those feelings.

My biggest fear when I gave up drinking was that my life would be boring, and that I would be boring. I worried that my friends wouldn't want to spend time with me anymore. Being new to a sober life, those fears haven't completely gone away, but I've

Finding Joy Within™

learnt to slowly enjoy socialising without alcohol. When I've been allowed to socialise during Covid times, I've been to BBQs, the pub, house parties, a UK break and restaurants. I have not yet sampled an abroad holiday, a big party or a nightclub – that is yet to come!

I can't take all the credit for this journey. I was blessed to have many Personal Development experts in my life and found the online alcohol support world to be a crucial part of my journey. I joined The Naked Mind Coaching Programme when I decided to quit alcohol. This programme, run by Annie Grace, re–educated me on the mental, physical and emotional effects of drinking and was an outlet when I found myself in emotional turmoil. This was almost every day in the initial stages!

It was only when I gave up the drink that I realised what a significant impact it was having on my life, and how much I had used it as a tool to stop me feeling anything. I didn't expect the rollercoaster ride that quitting alcohol has and is still giving me, but I don't regret my decision for one single moment given the things I have discovered about myself, my relationships and the life that I can create. Equally, nor do I regret the time I spent drinking, as I can't change the past and have some amazing memories of events and occasions, many where alcohol was involved.

It's been a year now since I initially quit alcohol. I am not saying I will never drink again, as that feels like too much pressure when I am still taking each day at a time, however I know for sure that I will not drink again until I know I can truly live a joyful life without the use of a substance. There have been many occasions, particularly after I hit one hundred days that I have thought, 'maybe I could just have one', but I know it's not right for me because I am still experiencing finding that joyful place every single day. I also know from others who have been on this journey, that it takes time, and can sometimes take a couple of years to achieve that state. So for now, I will continue with my new–found habits and rituals and continue to broaden my knowledge in my pursuit of happiness!

From speaking with others, I don't think the sort of relationship I had with alcohol is uncommon. I believe there are many people in the world, particularly after Covid, using alcohol to relieve stresses or to add interest to everyday life. If you feel the time is right now for you to make positive changes in your life, I hope my story gives you some inspiration that it's possible to live a joyful life by reaching within.

THE SHOW MUST GO ON

2016

21st November

I can smell the strong cinnamon fragrance of the freshly baked mince pies and the pine scent of the real Christmas tree. The room feels cosy. The sofa is covered in plump, plum cushions and cream, furry throws. The matching cream, thick, furry rug on the wooden floor feels like marshmallows when you walk on it and the twinkling Christmas lights illuminate the room. I'm in my front room with my amazing friends and family. The house is filled with laughter and love. I have a glass of Prosecco in hand (of course!) and Michael Bublé is singing, 'It's beginning to look a lot like Christmas'. I love Christmas – it's my favourite time of the year.

I'm chatting to Vicky – one of the most important people in my life for more than thirty years. Vicky has blonde hair, blue eyes and is always smiling, no matter what is going on in her life. She's always been my rock. We are talking about the plans we have for the festive period, which are all very exciting! A trip to Manchester Christmas markets, the Christmas party night at our local hotel and caroling in the pub on Christmas Day. I met my husband and many of my friends through the brass band when I was younger, and I love that Christmas reunites us through music.

As people start to depart, my joyous feeling begins to fade quickly. It's approaching 6pm, and I have a sick feeling in my stomach at the thought of what awaits me on the laptop. After I've tucked Emma, my beautiful 11–year–old daughter into bed, I log onto my laptop: perceived criticism, demands for work in short timescales, stress and anxiety, all of which I know will roll into the next week. I say to myself, 'Kath, it's not fair to land this on anyone else at short notice, so where can you find some more time from?' So, I can sacrifice time for myself, I can reduce my sleep, Glen (my husband) can take Emma to dancing and gymnastics and the list goes on. I manage to find about 15–20 hours, and think right it'll be okay – it's just a week. However, this wasn't just a week – it was years of the same pattern of behaviours.

For years I have struggled with anxiety, even though I am surrounded by the best family I could ever wish for, a truly amazing set of friends who are, to me, part of my family and without whom I couldn't function. I have my physical health, enough money to do most of the things I'd like to, a range of hobbies and interests which connect me with a variety of extremely interesting and lovely people and a great career. However, I am still struggling constantly with a sense of emptiness and anger at times and I can't understand why.

I have found that the busier I become, the more I am left feeling lonely, exhausted and overwhelmed. One of my oldest friends, Andre, always tells me I am trying to fit 28 hours of activities into 24 hours, which results in me being late to most places I go! I'm not able to fully value and appreciate the fantastic experiences I have and I'm generally run absolutely ragged! I consistently make promises to myself, which I then break, causing me to be angry and resentful. I'm afraid to say no to people, to set boundaries and stand up for myself and I feel weak and powerless which is making it difficult for me to communicate effectively with many people around me.

I think the reason for this is lack of self–worth. Whilst I am confident to try new things and meet new people, I don't necessarily value myself. I've never really felt loved (even though the number of people I have around me showing concern and love for me reflects a very different picture!) and I don't allow myself to feel anything but fear of being hurt or rejected.

Although I've always known that I use work to build up some of my self–esteem, I've only just started to realise how much I have come to depend on my career and recognition at work, to enable me to feel like a good person and to feel complete.

22nd November

It's 5am on Monday when my alarm goes off – as usual I check my emails before I get out of bed to see what's there.

Oh God... My heart sinks.

Kath – I need a report for the council leader for tomorrow; Kath– can you come and present at a meeting on Tuesday at 6pm; Kath – can you draft a board paper for close of play tomorrow –it's been missed off the agenda. Then to my next source of irritation for the day – Facebook! I see a Facebook post from her who I shall name as 'The Devil Wears Prada', telling the world about her amazing weekend and her amazing life! She looks after herself well: perfect nails, perfect make up, perfect hair, perfect figure and my comparititis is kicking in big time. She's everything I think I'm not and the chimp in my head is going crazy. It certainly doesn't look like she has a problem with her work life balance!

Over the next two hours, the pressure and anxiety within my head is building. My head feels like it's going to explode! Glen is talking to me but I'm not listening properly (God I'm a shit wife...). I'm just thinking about what I need to do in the next week. The TV is on, but I can't hear – it's all just white noise compared to the clarity inside my head of negative self – talk.

Kath – why can't you find time to at least put a bit of make up on? Kath – why can't you delegate? Kath – why can't you find the time to get to the gym and lose some weight? Kath – do you think you should be prioritising your home and family a bit more than your work? The noise goes on. My head is pounding. I feel sad, angry and upset, and all my childhood memories of being different, unconfident and disliked are flooding back to me, as they do on a daily basis. My memories of that little girl being sat in the window, looking at other children playing, whilst thinking 'why don't they want to play with me' and the feelings of sadness that come, overwhelm me. There is nothing that particularly triggers the memories; they are just always there, like a constant record in the background.

I drive to work, and as I enter the car park, I feel physically sick. I grit my teeth and clench my steering wheel. My stomach sinks and my heart starts to palpitate. I have been successful in my NHS career for years, however for the past few months I've really doubted myself in my director role from a confidence and competence perspective.

As I enter the Executive Team meeting, I know it's not going to be a pleasant experience. For about an hour and a half, the crazy flat–mate in my head is telling me what a shit job I am doing and that I need to work harder and try harder. I stand up from the desk to go to the toilet, to prevent myself from crying in public. The next memory I have is of me lying on the floor. In the next moment I can hear 'Kath, Kath– are you okay? Kath talk to me'. I'm on the floor, shaking, feeling very sick with all my colleagues surrounding me. I feel absolutely, bloody terrified, as I have never experienced anything like this in my life before. I am also slightly embarrassed thinking Oh My God, how gracefully did I fall as I had a skirt on!

23rd November

The day after I am in the Occupational Health Department with Florence, the nurse in a cold, clinical room, which matches my mood. Florence is lovely though. She has bright red hair, rosy cheeks, a bubbly personality and reminds me a little of my grandma. My grandma was warm and caring – I loved spending time with her, and she always made me feel special.

"So, tell me love what's going on for you?"

I pause, my chest tightens, as it has done most days for the past few months, and I start to sob uncontrollably.

"Come on love, talk to me."

After what feels like an eternity of silence...

"Florence, I just can't do anything right. I just feel like everyone's on my back all the time. I haven't got enough time to do anything that I want to do. I feel like I'm doing a shit job at work, I feel like I can't please anyone let alone myself. I feel like my boss thinks I'm doing a crap job. I feel like I'm a crap mum, a crap wife. I feel exhausted and I just can't see a way forward anymore. I just want to get off this rollercoaster. I want it all to stop!

There are not enough hours in the day – I don't know whether it's my exercise, my sleep, or time with my family that I'm going to have to sacrifice – I just want it all to stop. I've been working 70 hours a week for as long as I can remember, and I just can't see an end to it. I feel undervalued, I feel worthless and I just want it all to end."

"Kath, you're clearly very tired. I am going to sign you off for four weeks and I want you to go to your GP and seriously consider some antidepressants to lift your mood. It's not normal to feel this low."

"Antidepressants? Antidepressants? But I'm not depressed – I'm just tired!"

I know there is no point in arguing – I just need to take her advice.

As I sit in the hospital car park, I am mortified and I feel like a failure. I think I've only had about four days off sick in the 18 years I've worked for the NHS, but I know I don't have a choice. I'm not the person I thought I was – I am weaker than I thought I was. I've lost myself and I've let myself down at work, which is the only place where I feel I add any value. I feel worthless.

2017

4th January

I'm with Florence again in the Occupational Health Department.

"So Kath– how've you been?"

"I've been good, thanks Florence. I've enjoyed Christmas, I've started taking the antidepressants (said through gritted teeth…) and I'm ready to go back to work."

"That's brilliant! So tell me what you've been up to."

"Well, to be fair for the first couple of weeks I was so exhausted that I didn't get out of bed, but for the past couple of weeks, I've spent time with friends, I've done some things for myself and I'm ready and raring to go back."

"So Kath, what strategies have you put in place to look after yourself and to enjoy yourself?"

"Errr. Well. Err – I've not really got any strategies."

I'm thinking to myself – strategies for enjoyment, what the f*** is that? Fun – I don't do fun – I just do hard work!

"Well, unless you've done something to manage your well—being in the long term, I'm not really prepared to let you go back. Unless you've got some strategies to look after yourself I can't let you go back — I'll see you again in two weeks with a plan of what you're going to do."

That afternoon, I sit in my spare bedroom, my meditation room. The incense is burning and spiritual music is playing gently in the background, and I am thinking how the hell do I have a place in my house like this which oozes calm, positivity and serenity, yet I feel so stressed. I've got hundreds of books, CDs and magazines here telling me how to live a happy and fulfilled life, but I feel like I've not seriously committed to action after reading or listening to them.

Then I notice my diaries — about twenty of them — all from different years of my life. I begin to read them.

Age 37: A fuchsia pink journal embossed in gold flowers. Describing my ideal life — it's filled with love, passion, fun, hope and faith, but it all just feels like a pipe dream!

Age 34: My Buddha diary filled with reflections from my daily meditations. I learnt Transcendental Meditation with Lewis from Farnworth (he looked a bit like Geoffrey from Rainbow). Lewis was 60 and looked about 40 — it's known as the Botox effect of meditation, and I thought it worth a go just for that! Joking aside, this has been one of the things that has stayed with me since I learnt it and is vitally important for my mental stability. Although, some of my friends did question where I was going on a Saturday afternoon to someone's house in Farnworth with £500 cash for the course, a white handkerchief, a bowl of fruit and a bunch of fresh flowers

I feel happy with myself that I've managed to commit to meditation. I have actually trained to become a meditation teacher myself and have started running some classes in the community. Many people don't realise what meditation is. For me, it's a tool to press reboot when your mind is going round like the wheel of doom on the computer.

Exercise and food habits have been a little more 'loose' shall we say. Wanting that extra half hour in bed, the extra ice cream or glass, or two of wine has seemed slightly more appealing and at 40 I'm still using the same excuses I was years ago.

Age 27: A brown diary covered in musical notes – 'I just want to be happy' I look at the tear–stained pages and reconnect with the depths of my unhappiness at that time. I didn't realise then that it was only me who could make me happy – I was constantly looking for other people or material things to make me feel content.

The diaries go on. Every book I read, all I can see is a little girl in front of me. She looks sad, vulnerable and doesn't know where to turn for helpful advice and then I realise it's me – the young me. I didn't know where to look for advice and if I'm honest, I'm still not fully sure.

Emma, my daughter, who is my life's joy and inspiration comes running into the room. Mummy, Mummy I've made you a present. She hands me a shoebox with 'My Happy Box' written on it. A white box with pale green writing. It is typical of her kindness and I'm overwhelmed with emotion when I think about the consideration, compassion and understanding of a eleven–year–old.

I'm excited to see what's inside: medals from triathlons and the Manchester marathon, photographs of holidays and good times, pictures that Emma had drawn for me when she was younger, programmes from dance shows, singing reviews and amateur dramatics shows that I've been in. Where on earth had she found all this stuff?

I've no idea how on earth I had the confidence to do any of those things as an adult, given I've never danced or sang in my life before. One of the things I remember wanting to do, when I was younger, was to be an angel in the Christmas nativity. My mum was a music teacher at my primary school and felt it might appear as favouritism if I was picked to be an angel. What I now know, at eight years old, I interpreted this as I'm not pretty enough or good enough! Funny how small things like that stay with you.

I've done many creative things as I've got older with my besties. I've continued with my musical hobbies with my brass band friends, and Claire and I did a couple of Burlesque dancing shows at 180 Club in Tyldesley, though we did get a bit of grief for that from our partners, kids and friends.

Natalie and I starred in The Wedding Singer at St. Paul's Players in Adlington – I'm pushing to the back of my mind the fact that on the opening night during the opening dance, I tripped over my wedding dress in the first scene whilst all my friends were watching!

For the next two weeks, I reflect regularly on what has brought me to this position. I recognise that I am making too many sacrifices at home. I want to be the person that takes Em to her hobbies every week. I want to be the person that cooks tea, I want to be the person that puts Em to bed at night. I want to spend time with my husband and I want to do stuff that I enjoy. On the other hand, I feel guilt that I might look like I'm not pulling my weight and setting a bad example in the office to my team if I'm not physically present and staying at work until at least 6pm each evening and then making sure that I log back in and carry on working later in the evening when I'm at home too.

I am investing significant amounts of personal time and money in therapy, to try and adjust my thought processes to be more positive, confident and compassionate to myself. However, I'm not putting things into practice properly. During my period of sickness, I realise that I can only control what I can control, which needs to be the focus of my recovery. Some of this links to how I'm prioritising my time in the week at work, how I'm prioritising my personal time and how I'm reacting to certain situations. I am definitely stuck in negative and fear thinking.

19th September

I'm entering the Thistle Hotel in Manchester Airport, Terminal 3. It's a single storey building on the airport Ring Road – a bit soulless, you know, like many of these airport hotels are.

As I enter the conference room, with its dark red and cream swirling carpet, wood–paneled walls and strong scent of Jo Malone Pomegranate Noir fragrance, the atmosphere immediately changes. The energy in this room feels so different to anything I've felt in a long time. I feel uplifted immediately! The music is pumping out at nightclub volume. A huge screen faces me, with a motivational video of Will Smith playing. People are dancing, singing and whooping. It's 9am and not a drop of alcohol in sight! What the hell is this place?

As I take my seat, I feel excited, but a little intimidated as well, if I'm honest. I notice people dotted around the room dressed in black T–shirts, with a yellow lightning strike plastered on the back of them and the words 'Power to Achieve'! What's striking about these people, is how they all look so damned happy, which is so different to how I feel most days.

'Ladies and gentlemen, please welcome to the stage...Mr Andy Harrington!' This guy runs onto the stage to massive whoops and applause! He's smartly dressed, with a southern accent (being a Northerner I didn't hold that against him). He's quite short, but with amazing white teeth! I've never heard of Andy before, however with Tony Robbins, Les Brown and Brendon Burchard as my new 'virtual' best friends, clearly Facebook thinks I will like him!

And they are right – I instantly like him. There is something engaging and charismatic about him, but also something that feels genuine about his passion in life to help people.

I'm sat next to lovely Yvette. She's very pretty, slim, with long brown hair and wearing oval glasses.

Part way through the day, we are in the middle of a transformational process. The lights in the room are turning red – Andy is asking me (well obviously not just me, but I felt like he was talking to just me), if you die today, what dreams would die with you?

"Yvette, what dreams would die with you?"

"Well Kath, being the next Charlie Dimmock, of course – I'm here to grow my gardening business."

"Oh...

"What about you then Kath?"

"Erm – I don't know. Dreams – I've never really had dreams. I just know about working hard for a living."

My mind flashes back to November 2016.

As I sit with Yvette, I ask myself some questions. Have things changed that much for me? Do I love my life now? Do I know my reason for being? A strong, deep, resounding 'NO' echoes around in my head.

I spend the rest of the weekend breaking through wooden blocks and bending metal rods with my throat (I kid you not). There is something truly inspiring and charismatic about this group of people and I want to be part of this tribe.

Andy pitches his Professional Speakers University, which apparently can turn you into a world–class speaker or author! I have no interest in speaking, as a complete introvert, it is my worst nightmare! In that moment, I feel a passionately strong connection to writing a book and realise it is something I've always wanted to do! Best selling author – here I come!

"There's always a reason to smile,
you just have to find it."

- De Philosopher DJ Kyos

amazon.co.uk®

A gift from **Love emma xxx**

My friends book for you mummy bear
From Love emma xxx

Gift note included with **Finding Joy WithinTM - The Book (How To Live Your Life With Presence, Purpose And Authenticity)**

U1yTPHVY9/-1 of 1-/premium-uk/0 A3

Packing slip for

Your order of 22 April 2022
Order ID 206-3485299-8627505

Packing slip number U1yTPHVY9
Shipping date 22 April 2022

Qty.	Order Summary	Bin
1	Finding Joy WithinTM - The Book (How To Live Your Life With Presence, Purpose And Authenticity) Paperback. Wynne-Jones, Kath. B09TZ1QD88 : B09TZ1QD88: 9798425241344	

We hope you enjoy your gift, and we'd love to see you soon at www.amazon.co.uk

0/U1yTPHVY9/-1 of 1-//LH-MAN8/premium-uk/0/0423-21:00/0423-03:31 Pack Type : A3

FIGHT SONG

2019

25th May

It's 3am and I'm standing against the aged, wooden kitchen unit, clutching a crystal tumbler filled with brandy. I can feel the cold, slate floor beneath my feet.

The kitchen is a mess, broken glass and crockery everywhere. The room is a mess, my life is a mess and I'm a mess.

Just hours prior, the atmosphere was so different. We were getting ready for our annual camping trip to Pooley Bridge with our friends. Me and my beautiful daughter Emma were singing excitedly to One Direction, whilst we were packing our things. She was getting together her clothes, beauty products and her fake tan, whilst I was packing the snacks, the food and most importantly, the wine and the gin! ☺ It was one of those times where you think you're going for a month rather than a week, with the amount of stuff that you pack!

And then it all changed...

My husband, my childhood sweetheart of 26 years, about 5 ft 8, bald head and a beard entered the room.

"Kath we need to talk."

This doesn't sound great...

"We're not going on holiday tomorrow."

"What do you mean we're not going on holiday? Of course we're going on holiday. I've spent all night packing the camper van."

"No, we're not going on holiday," as he gestures his finger between the two of us.

"But, but I don't understand... What, what are you trying to tell me?"

"Kath, I'm so sorry. I'm telling you that this isn't working and I want a separation."

At the top of my voice, I am shouting and sobbing, "SORRY! SORRY! WHAT DO YOU MEAN YOU'RE SORRY?"

"I've been saying for ages that things weren't right and we needed to sort stuff out and you kept telling me it was all in my head and now you're telling me you want to separate."

"I don't understand...I don't understand...I just DON'T understand."

"WHY couldn't you have been honest with me sooner?"

"I love you – what am I going to do without you?"

"What are we going to tell Emma?"

"I can't be on my own – I won't survive on my own!"

"What are we going to tell our friends?"

"What are we going to tell our parents?"

"Was it all my fault?"

"I just don't understand...?"

Have you ever experienced a time like that? In an instant, your life changed?

Before I knew it, I had smashed everything on the surfaces in the kitchen – the plates, the crockery, and the glasses. I was filled with rage in a way I've never been in my entire life. This was totally out of character for me, as I am normally a very quiet, calm and peaceful person.

The thing was, I wasn't really angry with him, well I was a bit...I was more angry with myself. How often and for how long had I contained my sense of knowing something wasn't right? I was angry at the small things I'd ignored – something that wasn't right in a friendship, or problems at work. And I was angry at the big things I had ignored – the fact I knew I was losing myself for many years that led me to an emotional breakdown and the fact that I knew there was something wrong in my marriage, but I didn't know how to deal with it.

Have you ever had a time in your life when everything appears broken in front of you and you have no idea how to rebuild it?

We tried for three months to salvage our marriage. In the end I think we both recognised that the best thing for us and for Emma, was for us to separate.

4ᵗʰ September

This is the saddest day of my life. There is no going back, and I take my wedding and engagement rings off. I am officially separating from Glen and I am absolutely, f****** heartbroken. If I'm honest, when he told me he wanted a separation in May, I didn't think he meant it, but clearly he did. I can still see the tan line from where my ring had been during my two week summer holiday in Lanzarote in August. Damn it, I could do without that f****** reminder every day!

I'm 44, and I've no idea how I'm supposed to be on my own. I have never been on my own in my life before – I've been with Glen since childhood sweethearts at 16. He has been part of my whole identity, and from feeling lonely throughout my life, he was my saviour. The only thing that still gives me hope is that I have been to Lanzarote with Em and our friends, without Glen and we had a lovely time for a large part of the holiday. Maybe there is hope for me?

19ᵗʰ September

I'm at a beautiful barn in Huddersfield, on my latest personal development course – the Find Your Why Masterclass. Find Your Why does pretty much what it says on the tin. For years I've been searching, trying to find my true purpose in life. I know I'm here to make a difference in the world, I just don't know what that looks like. The sun is streaming through the windows, I'm sitting on the brown leather sofa clutching a cup of coffee and I can hear the babbling brook at the bottom of the garden. Cheryl is stood opposite me, pen poised on the flip chart. She's laughing, her blonde hair in plaits and her glasses pushed to the end of her nose. Marion is sat next to me, her legs crossed underneath her, looking as though she is about to start a meditation session.

I can feel her positive energy reaching out to me. I met Cheryl and Marion at the Professional Speakers Academy and both of these people have been a huge support and inspiration to me over recent weeks. But still, all I can see in front of me is that I am a failure...

In the style of Jeremy Paxman, Cheryl is interrogating me about my successes. I'm not able to see many.

"Right, come on then Kath, you are a director in the NHS. You must have overcome some challenges to succeed in your career."

"Err... yep okay. I probably have done some stuff I'm proud of..."

"Well, I used to work excessive hours and was constantly connected to my emails and my phone, because it was the only place I got any self–worth. I had a nervous breakdown in 2016, which made me re–evaluate things. Now, I know I do a good job, I'm more productive and have a good work–life balance."

Cheryl looks at me inquisitively, "Okay, what else?"

"Err... I've completed a marathon and a couple of triathlons. And I've got enough professional certificates to decorate the downstairs of my house. When I commit to something, I will put all my effort into it to achieve what I set out to do."

"I've got a brilliant relationship with my daughter and I know I have friends and family who care about me."

Cheryl writes down the topics I have told her.

"So Kath, what can you see in front of you? What's the common connection?"

"Erm, me...?"

"Yep, no shit Sherlock. What else?"

Work

Achievements

Relationships

As I study closer, the word WAR appears in front of me. I realise I have been at WAR with myself my entire life. Tears rolled down my cheeks. Nothing I ever did was good enough by my standards: the next qualification, the next promotion, the next event. I've never stopped to celebrate my accomplishments or to appreciate that I am a good kind person, without all of that. I rarely feel happy and content in the moment of any of my successes. I'm always onto the next thing.

I am grateful for everybody and everything in my life. I am not grateful for me and I don't value myself at all. My resilience is strong, to enable me to keep going with everything, however, my levels of joy and my self–esteem are at rock bottom.

The vulnerable little girl, my eight–year–old self, appears again in front of me, as she did back in 2016, instead, now she's really angry – "How can you not have seen me? How can you have worked me so hard and not appreciated me? You've not valued me – you've looked at other people and been jealous of them and not seen what you had all along – you have never acknowledged me! All you have done is drive me into the ground. Why have you never seen me?"

And then it hits me – I've been constantly looking for approval from other people, and for others to accept me. I've always done what people expect of me, continuously looking for people to value me, yet I've never been able to value myself. This is my realisation that I have to make changes, not just for myself, but as a role model to Emma; to show her that the value you feel in life, starts with the value you feel inside and for yourself.

I begin to realise that I have the power within me to create the life I want to lead.

14th October

I knew this day would come ever since the time my marriage ended. The day I have been dreading. The day I must face my biggest fear, (or so I thought). All week, the anxiety in my body has been escalating and I'm ashamed of how I reacted to Emma this morning, as I felt less in control of my emotions than normal. Getting irritated with her in the car about being late for school and not having packed her bags quickly enough. None of this was her fault. It was because I couldn't manage my insecurities well enough. Tonight will be my first night away from Emma since the separation. She is staying at her Dad's new house for the first time and it's the first day I find myself truly alone.

For as long as I can remember, I have always feared being on my own, but never understood why. Today, I understand. I am able to label my fear and my reality of being abandoned. I feel alone, isolated and like I have nobody in the world by my side. From a very young age, I never felt like I fitted in. I was always the odd one out at school. Being an only child and not having siblings to play with, I had quite a lonely childhood. I wasn't really invited to play with others and I didn't have the confidence to join in myself. The brass band circle, where I met Glen, accepted me. When I joined the band, I felt like at last I belonged somewhere and with someone, which has made our separation even harder. Now, it seems like I have lost everything that helps me to feel secure and gives me a sense of belonging.

Since my realisation at the Find Your Why Masterclass, of how much at WAR I have been with myself, I'm trying to treat myself with compassion, kindness and care. It can be a challenging process when you've lived with a crazy lodger in your head for 43

Finding Joy Within™

29

years. Quietening her negative voice is not going to happen overnight. I am making small strides to speak kindly to myself and see the positive opportunities in difficult situations. As I work my way through this marital separation, to the best outcome for us all, I am constantly faced with the light and dark sides of change.

Sometimes I feel the changes day to day, hour to hour or minute to minute, depending upon external things that are happening, my state of mind and the support I have around me. I am holding onto the fact that I can only face the light if I live in darkness for a while. I know that change always has two sides. Numerous people have been telling me that writing will help me heal. I'm not sure, if I'm honest. Here goes with my first blog:

The Dark: Why me? The Light: This happened for a higher purpose that will, one day, become clear to me.

The Dark: I need to control everything to get through this. The Light: Where do I need to put my trust and faith to get me through this?

The Dark: I don't understand what's going on. The Light: I don't have to understand what's going on – one day I will understand why this happened.

The Dark: I'm weak and I can't get through this. The Light: This experience will make me a stronger, more resilient person.

The Dark: It's all my fault, I'm mad and angry with myself for not being different, to be able to make this relationship work. The Light: I am enough. I have good qualities and it takes two for a relationship to fail.

The Dark: I'm angry at the situation and I don't deserve this. The Light: What lessons does the universe feel I need to learn through and from this experience?

Finding Joy Within™

The Dark: Why is no one else in my family feeling the same amount of pain, is it because they don't care? The Light: Everybody has their own process – it doesn't mean they don't care, we all have our own way of dealing with things.

The Dark: How will this ever be okay? The Light: It will be okay in the end. If it's not okay; it's not the end.

13th December

I'm standing on a 6ft wide, red, velvet circle, with a 10ft high, red, glitter shoe on my right, the distinctive, big, red T. E. D. letters to my left and what seems like thousands of people facing me in the audience. I'm approaching the last few minutes of my TEDx talk on resilience and sharing what I believe from my own research, education and experience are the Three Key Factors of Resilience.

"I believe the 3 Fs of Resilience are:

1. Feelings: Noticing and accepting your feelings, whether they be good or bad. If we suppress negative emotions, they can make us ill. If we don't take time to reflect on the big and small positive things that happen in our lives, they can sometimes pass us by.

2. Focus: Placing your focus on the future and knowing what you can do to change your mental state if you find you are in a funk. I know that going for a run, even though I may not always want to do it, will, almost always, make me feel better. What is it that you do that changes your emotional state?

3. Friendships: Who are the people you can go to who accept you unconditionally, will not judge you and will inspire you to become the best you can be? Are you prioritising those uplifting people, or are you focusing on the people who drain you? The best piece of advice someone gave me was, if you wouldn't go to someone for advice; then don't listen to their criticisms.

"I believe resilience is like the Japanese art of Kintsugi. When pottery breaks, it's not thrown away, it is carefully glued together and the cracks are mended and adorned with gold to make it more beautiful. I believe as human beings, that each one of the challenges we face in our lives is represented by the gold in that artwork. Each time we overcome a challenge, we become more beautiful and resilient human beings."

The audience are clapping and cheering and I am overcome with a sense of pride that I have never felt in my life before.

The happiest day of my life was the day that Emma was born, closely followed by my wedding day. However, I couldn't take sole responsibility for my happiness on either of those occasions.

Today, I am proud of me and I know that the sense of satisfaction I have is a result of the effort I have put in to recreate my life positively.

I could so easily still have been crying on the kitchen floor holding a bottle of wine. Instead, I knew I had to grow as a person to be a positive role model to my daughter and others. Now, don't get me wrong, it hasn't been an easy journey over the past six months. There have been many days when I have cried, looked for answers that aren't there, asked myself, what did I do wrong, was it my fault, or was it because I had a career? None of these were helpful questions. It has taken many different people who believed in me, when I didn't believe in myself, to build my confidence and momentum, to help me ask myself these useful questions. I am truly grateful to Cheryl for her support over the past few months and for giving me this opportunity to become a TEDx Speaker!

31st December

My last diary entry of the year, as I sit on the balcony of our skiing chalet in Chamonix looking out towards Mont Blanc. I am so grateful to Simone for arranging this trip and all the other lovely holidays we have had this year.

Dear 2019, you were interesting...

• You gave me a divorce and the associated heartbreak, loneliness, guilt, shame and unworthiness that went with it.

• You gave me leadership struggles, so I believed I was not having any beneficial impact on people's lives.

• You enabled me to connect at a deeper level with my daughter and friends, in a way I didn't think possible.

• You provided me with an opportunity to travel with Emma and my friends and experience new parts of the world. If you had told me I would be going on our family holiday to Lanzarote, as a single mum with Emma and our friends and was going to have the most amazing time ever. Or that I would be in Dubai coaching people how to be a better version of themselves, I wouldn't have believed you.

• You supported me in becoming an ACE mentor for the Professional Speakers Academy (I became an Andy Harrington fan!) I became a TEDx speaker and shared what I am passionate about with the world.

• As Emma and I have settled into our new life, I have felt life return to me. I feel alive. I have opportunities before me and I can do, or be, anything I want to be.

I am thankful for you because...

Finding Joy Within™

• You didn't just hand me a separation from my husband. You helped me feel whole on my own, although this is an ongoing journey.

• You didn't make me lose hope in love.

• You didn't overwhelm my family with trauma.

• You've helped me begin to express myself.

• You've guided me to people, support and communities who will help me grow.

• You've let me experience new things, with many more to come in 2020.

• You've helped me to love and accept myself and those around me, in a way that I never could before.

In 2020, I want to:

• Express myself fully.

• Be the best mum I can be to Em and my doggies.

• Take full responsibility for my mental, physical, emotional and spiritual health by putting in place healthy daily habits (sounds familiar...)

• Spend time with family and friends doing things that don't cost lots of money and feed my body, mind and spirit. (New insert: little did I know that would be on Zoom every Saturday night because there's nowhere else to go!)

• Travel to new parts of the world. (New insert: I think the furthest I got was Rivington Beach, five miles away from my house!)

• Become a best–selling author, world–class speaker, start my own business and launch my online products and events. (New insert: this is taking me a little longer than I thought to feel authentic.)

• Focus on being in the present and enjoying the now, rather than living in the past or the future.

• Be the best leader I can be, by spending my time and energy in places where I can have a positive impact.

• Create a home environment that supports me and Em emotionally, physically and spiritually.

• Create opportunities for joy, fun and expressing my creativity each day.

Goodbye, 2019! X

"Life isn't about waiting for the storm to pass...It's about learning to dance in the rain"

- Vivian Greene

BROKEN AND BEAUTIFUL

2020

5th January

New Year – new start! Time to create my manifestation board!

You may have heard of vision boards and manifesting. Vision boards are a way of dreaming, seeing and feeling the life you would like to live. Quite frankly, this couldn't be further away from how I've lived my life previously! However, since I watched The Secret, I have become a massive believer in them. The theory behind a vision board is that if you put your attention on the images in your vision board, the energy of that thing will be more prominent in your awareness and you will be more open to receiving (or so Tony Robbins tells me).

Tony has also educated me that the universe responds to both your positive and negative thoughts. If you look for reasons to support your thoughts on why you are having a terrible day, you'll keep attracting situations to prove you right. But if you surround yourself with the things you want to experience, the more likely you are to actually experience those things in your life. Taking that a step further, if you believe that what you dream of, you have already achieved, you can trick your mind

into believing that it's already happened, making it even more likely to occur! What a fabulous prospect!

As Tony says, "Energy flows where attention goes."

I create my vision board and place it in the 'abundance' area of my home. I have recently started to study Feng Shui with Hannah, which is about the energy you are creating in your home.

I have always known that my environment has an important role to play in my well–being. What I am seeing, hearing and experiencing at any moment is not only changing my mood, but also how my body and immune system function. However, I've not made many physical changes in my home before.

If you haven't come across it before, feng shui is the Chinese practice of creating balance with the natural world in our interior spaces. It uses energy forces to create harmony between us and our environment. It's not about changing the structure of your home but making small changes that can have a significant impact on your energy levels.

There are five elements that can be present in our homes: earth, wood, fire, water, and metal, either physically or symbolically. Based on a number of factors, including our date of birth, we all have our own element. The idea of feng shui is to balance the elements, which support you and the flow of your home, based on the directions of energy flowing in and out of it. For example, people with anger issues should be wary of having too many fire elements as part of their decor. Conversely, personality types lacking motivation should include more of the fire element in their homes to give them motivation.

I am not a feng shui expert, but after I sought guidance from a practitioner, Hannah, there were ten things I changed in my home:

1. I got rid of a Buddha figurine in my garden that had cracked from the weather and was giving sad and lonely vibes. She was actually on the blessing spot in my house, therefore driving some of the sad energy into the home.

2. I decluttered everywhere, and I now have an ongoing cycle of decluttering.

3. I paired up all of my hearts, as you should never have a single heart displayed on its own.

4. I replaced my fake plants with real ones (my only exception is where the temperature is too hot in rooms for me to be a good plant mum).

5. I put salt lamps in rooms in my home where I needed more fire elements to support my energy.

6. I made sure I loved everything I had in my home and if I didn't, I got rid of it – including some of the contents of my wardrobe.

7. I put artwork, pictures and plants in my hall that inspire me as I enter and leave our home.

8. I had an initial sage smudging ritual, which I now repeat on a regular basis.

9. I placed weights under furniture in the rooms that needed more metal energy. I have to be honest, if anyone ever moves a sofa and finds my 33kg weight plates underneath it, I get a few odd looks. ☺

10. I created my vision manifestation board and placed it in my 'abundance' area.

From these changes and redecorating my home with colours that suited the energy and inspire me, I feel much more relaxed and supported in my home. Prior to this, I felt quite restricted. Part of this was because there was little fire energy anywhere in the house, which is what I need to support my energy levels.

Each morning, before I leave home, I spend a few minutes looking at my vision manifestation board and imagine I am already doing or receiving those things to set me up for the day.

I am finding that picturing what my ideal day, week and year looks like is helping me to think positively. I am starting to dream of things I want to do, places I want to travel to, relationships I want to experience and the impact I want to have in the world. Imagining what I will be seeing, hearing, feeling and sensing is starting to bring me alive. This is something I haven't done in my life before.

Vishen Lakhiani, author and CEO of Mindvalley, tells me there are three important questions you need to ask yourself, to identify your goals and these include:

• Experiences: What experiences do I want to feel?

• Growth: How do I want to grow?

• Contribution: How do I want to contribute?

The Dalai Lama once said, if you want to be happy, you need to learn to make people happy. This relates to how you want to give to your family, your friends, your community, your employer and the planet. This resonates with me greatly.

All of these perspectives have been genuinely valuable for me in considering the design of my beautiful life.

25th January

Swipe right, swipe left – this is a whole other world! Quite frankly, this online dating world could be another full–time job, that I'm not sure I am ready for. I think I am reacting to the fact that my ex–husband has a new girlfriend. Although, I know there is no way I'm ready for another relationship. My confidence in myself is growing, although I don't think I can handle the brutality of the online dating world just yet! I also know that I need time on my own, time to heal and to start believing in myself, trusting myself and loving myself, knowing that a new partner will appear when the time is right. Elite Singles and Bumble apps – delete!

18th April

Today would have been my 22nd wedding anniversary. I should be in Amsterdam (escaping if I'm honest!), but instead, I am in the boardroom of the hospital. My anxiety levels are through the roof with the emotions of the day. This is my fifth week of fourteen–hour days, trying to be a good mum, supporting homeschooling, not knowing how to switch off and feeling challenged with everything that Covid is presenting me with at work and at home.

I'm now in a role coupled with the added pressure of Covid which means I have to be in the hospital 8am – 8pm and then travelling an hour either way.

My Covid experience is different to some of my friends. It hasn't given me much time for reflection. It's been a time for working extremely hard and trying to support the NHS in the best way I can. Covid has really challenged all the positives I put in place and caused a lot of these positives to go to sh*t. However, I am grateful that I can still work. I am grateful for the Thursday night clap and seeing my neighbours from a distance and if I'm honest, I'm very grateful for the chance it gives me to drink Prosecco on my doorstep with my neighbours!...and thus can give myself permission for a little evening reward for all the hours I'm working and plates I'm trying to keep spinning, whilst I continue riding on this massive and unknown wave of what is next to come with Covid. I am grateful for friends who have brought me wine, chocolates and flowers and I am grateful for the fabulous team I work with.

But my head is spinning trying to balance the different responsibilities of life. I'm feeling a little envious of not being able to press the pause button like many of the world at this time and I am seriously struggling facing the emotions of the fact that I am not celebrating our wedding anniversary and I never will again.

Finding Joy Within™

But I know that this too shall pass. I can't stop thinking that just two years ago we were in Venice and sailing down the canals on a gondola. My life seemed perfect! A far cry from today.

3rd May

About a week ago, I realised how tired I was and how disconnected I'd become, in those relationships that are important to me.

Normally my daily routine is:

• Wake up and write my gratitude diary at 6am.

• Meditate for 30 minutes.

• Get ready for work and have my breakfast.

• Make sure the dogs and Emma are sorted for the day and home schooling!

I'd like exercise to be on there, but quite frankly, I just don't have time at the moment other than short dog walks!

Over recent weeks, due to work and home pressures, I've sacrificed my morning routine, in favour of other things – notably scrolling through Facebook late at night and first thing in the morning, which is not adding any value to my life and I know it's got me into trouble before (2016). I'm still meditating, but probably every other day, rather than every day.

I take some time to remind myself of why I have my gratitude and meditation practice. I know that when I am struggling with something, re–educating myself of the benefits and my why for doing something will get me back into action.

Gratitude

My gratitude practice is often the first thing to slip in my routine when I am short on time. I know the science and importance of it in all major philosophies, religions, and schools of thought. Many studies have shown that people who practice gratitude experience better mental and physical health. We only have a limited amount of focus, so when you are able to be appreciative of what you have, your brain is unable to give life and energy to thoughts about what you don't have.

I love Germany Kent's quote, "It's a funny thing about life, once you begin to take note of the things you are grateful for, you begin to lose sight of the things that you lack."

Part of our problems come from our expectations and if that experience doesn't match our expectations, then we expose a gap that leads to unhappiness. And that's when you get left with that feeling of upset.

When I was feeling low a few years ago, somebody told me to write a list of three things I was grateful for every day. At first, I felt a bit like I was going through the motions and saying thank you for the big things, like my home, my health and my family and friends and I didn't really feel it. When I started to dial into the detail of the gratitude, of the small things, like the smell of a cup of coffee, feeling the sunshine on my face, or a conversation with a friend, it made me feel an intrinsic sense of peace and happiness that I had so infrequently experienced before. I know I need to set my gratitude practice from the heart back into place as it's so beneficial for me when I do.

Meditation

I'm so passionate about this topic, which led me to train as a meditation teacher with the British School of Meditation in 2018. I believe meditation is vital to stress–free living. I hope you can indulge me to share some of the science behind it and my personal experiences

A regular meditation practice has been an important part of me growing as a person. I know if I don't meditate each day, my mind starts to get very chaotic and I start to lose my sense of grounding (as I have now). I don't meditate in the same place, or in the same way every day, but I do spend ten minutes meditating every morning to start my day in a positive way. Multi–tasking is an issue for me and I need to control myself to only do one thing at once. Meditation has helped me to become more aware and in control of this. It's also been a good way for me to become more aware of my thoughts and emotions through my daily practice.

I learnt Transcendental Meditation (TM) a few years ago, which you do for twenty minutes twice a day. This was genuinely beneficial for me, but I started to be short of time for my practice, especially as a single mum. As I am writing this, I am thinking about what my teacher Lewis said to me, "Kath, if you can't find time to meditate for forty minutes, you need to meditate for an hour." Perhaps I need to take his advice a little more seriously right now…

Ellen Langer's research revealed that by paying attention to what is going on around us, instead of operating on autopilot, can reduce stress, unlock creativity and boost performance. Mindfulness and meditation have many similarities and can overlap; however, these are not exactly the same. Mindfulness is about having non–judgemental, present–moment awareness. That said, a regular meditation practice can increase your potential of being more mindful. There is now a vast amount of research which shows the positive effects of meditation on the brain. Just twenty minutes of meditation per day for three months can have significant impact on your brain functioning. MRI scans have shown that, after ten minutes of meditation from somebody who has been practising for three months, you can see brain activity massively reduced. This doesn't only impact on how you function and react, it also impacts on cardiovascular disease and other stress–related illnesses.

People who meditate regularly, have been shown to feel less anxiety and depression due to increases in serotonin during meditation. They also report that they experience more enjoyment and appreciation of life and that their relationships with others are improved. Establishing a regular meditation practice, along with exercise, was the key to enabling me to come off antidepressants painlessly at the end of 2018.

Sharon Salzberg, a leading expert in the field, describes meditation as: training our attention so that we can be more aware, not only of our own inner workings but also of what's happening around us in the here and now. Once we see clearly what's going on in the moment, we can then choose whether, and how, to act on what we are seeing.

Research regarding meditation has also been conducted both in smaller and bigger companies. Alongside physical health benefits, regular TM meditators also improved significantly (3 months into practice) on such crucial measures as:

• Effectiveness

• Leadership abilities

• Job satisfaction

• Professional relationships.

Numerous studies with students at all levels of their educational path (primary school, middle school, college, universities etc.) have also demonstrated that someone practising TM meditation benefits from:

• Increases in general intellectual and cognitive performance

• Positive impact on academic test results

• Reduced negative school behaviour (absenteeism, infractions)

• Reduced school–related stress, anxiety and depression

Many people who have learned to meditate have reported having an improved quality of sleep, as meditation can help you to become much calmer all of the time. As the meditation process clears the mind, it has also been linked to improved concentration levels.

Whenever we get upset or say something we regret, it's a sign that our amygdala (our brain's fight or flight response) has been hijacked. The key to resilience is how quickly we recover from that state. From a study by the University of Massachusetts, after eight weeks of practicing mindfulness meditation for thirty minutes a day, the employees of the institution had increased their left brain activity, which helped them recover from stress, and had got them more in touch with what they love about their work.

There is a famous story, though the author is unknown, about the impact of stress if we don't let go of it.

One day, a lecturer walked around a room while teaching stress management to an audience. As she raised a glass of water, everyone expected they'd be asked the "half empty or half full" question. Instead, with a smile on her face, she inquired, "How heavy is this glass of water?" The answers called out ranged from eight to twenty ounces. She replied, "The absolute weight doesn't matter. It depends on how long I hold it. If I hold it for a minute, it's not a problem. If I hold it for an hour, I'll have an ache in my arm. If I hold it for a day, my arm will feel numb and paralysed. In each case, the weight of the glass doesn't change, but the longer I hold it, the heavier it becomes."

She continued, "The stresses and worries in life are like that glass of water. Think about them for a while and nothing happens. Think about them a bit longer and they begin to hurt. And if you think about them all day long, you will feel paralysed – incapable of doing anything. It's important to remember to let go of your stresses. Remember to put the glass down!"

As well as helping to build my resilience and a deeper sense of peace, meditation has also helped to prevent me from doing rash things, such as speaking harshly to myself and others, becoming upset, or responding too quickly, particularly to emails. If I find my stress levels rising, for whatever reason, e.g. responding to perceived criticism or performing under pressure, I just take a few seconds to focus on my breathing and visualise a positive situation that brings me back into the present.

When we are in our thoughts, we can only ever be in the past, thinking about what has happened, or in the future, thinking about what might happen, or things we would like to do. If we are in the present moment we don't have thoughts – we are just where we are now.

Just because I'm so passionate about meditation, I'd like to share a couple of ideas for you that I practise myself:

• When you first wake up, spend a couple of minutes focusing on your breath. This could be followed by a ten–minute meditation if you wish. It has been found that we release the most stress hormones within a few minutes of waking, which is when many of us may reach for our phones, or spend minutes of dread thinking about what the day has in store, rather than fully grounding ourselves

• If you find yourself getting stressed during the day, take a break somewhere quiet and focus your attention on your breath or something else to take your focus away from what is distracting/upsetting you. As thoughts appear, bring your focus back to your breath and let the thoughts disappear like clouds in the sky.

• Go about your day with focus and awareness. Focus on what you are doing and notice thoughts and feelings as they arise. In this way, mindfulness helps to increase effectiveness and creativity. Focus on what's important, not what's easy. Emails have an ability to seduce us, because completing tasks releases dopamine, the pleasure hormone. However, avoiding your inbox first thing can keep you away from distractions that can disrupt your day.

• At the end of your working day, give yourself a few minutes to just 'be' without any distractions. This is even more important now with the number of people currently home working and not having the physical separation of work and home.

• Consider a short meditation before you go to bed.

I feel that meditation makes me a more positive, self-aware, resilient and caring human being. I also believe it makes me a more effective leader, as it helps me see the bigger picture by taking some time to make space for clarity of mind. Anyway, I hope I haven't bored you with this. I could talk for hours on the topic! But I do find it helpful to remind myself of why I meditate, especially if my practice is starting to lapse.

18th May

A couple of weeks after setting my morning routine back in place and doing the things that keep me well, I am feeling so much better and I know this has to be my priority to enable me to be there for others.

Kindness is the theme for Mental Health Awareness Week this month. There has been so much kindness shown across our communities in recent weeks and months, which I hope will long continue. People are shopping for each other, taking the time to ring or FaceTime people who are on their own, lending technology so that people can stay connected, donating food and other items to those who need it.

In my health and care organisation, I have seen so many moving stories of people and teams going above and beyond, to give compassionate care to patients and service users. Teams are coming together and working together in ways that we could have only dreamed of twelve months ago. Through this pandemic, there has been more collaboration across teams and organisations than I have ever seen in my career before in the NHS, because we have all been working to one purpose. I hope this will last!

I have felt humbled, how people working across health and social care nationally, have continued to deliver wonderful care for our population and helped to save lives. Despite the many challenges of home–schooling, uncertainties around household incomes and the loneliness that themselves, friends or family may have been facing. Whilst there have been tragedies of this pandemic, I hope that the positive new ways of delivering care, and that the spirit of gratitude, compassion and kindness remains long after the lockdown. Amid fear, there is also community, support and

Finding Joy Within™

hope. However, I'm not sure things will ever return to 'normal' either, in our personal or professional lives.

30th May

It's a beautiful Saturday morning! I'm standing in the kitchen. The sun is streaming through the windows and the birds are singing. We've had an amazing week over half term with our amazing support bubble the Leadbeaters! Canoeing on Chorley Canal and a picnic on Rivington Beach, not quite a holiday village in Turkey, but we've been blessed with sunshine and good times. ☺

Despite it being beautiful outside, I'm feeling like shit on the inside. I feel sluggish. I feel tired. I just can't be bothered. I am knackered and my heart is still racing as fast as it was at 3am this morning! I look at the pictures from the day before and I look horrific! My skin is red like a lobster with white sun glass marks because I didn't protect myself with enough suncream. My eyes look sad and my stomach is bloated like a balloon.

Have you ever heard the song Ten Green Bottles? Well, there were ten green bottles on my kitchen unit that day and not the ones you would have had at school! From the five days previous, seven Prosecco, two rosé and one large gin. I gave up drinking during weekdays in 2016, until the Thursday night claps for the NHS started in 2020. After that, I decided that Thursday to Sunday drinking was allowed. I'm cutting myself a bit of slack today as it's the holidays and telling myself it's ok, I'm allowed to drink during the week...but for f*** sake this is ridiculous and I feel like shit. Something needs to change.

I'm terrified! Drinking has been my crutch since I've been a teenager. I know it needs to stop. I've known this for a while, I've just not wanted to accept it. You see, I convince myself, it's not that I've truly been drinking, because I'm socialising. I've been drinking when I got home because I was lonely or stressed. Fizz has been my constant companion, since my separation. I know I have to face my fears and quit.

I click on the button 'Sign Up'...and in an instant I'm registered with the Naked Mind Coaching Programme to start tomorrow.

"To be human is to be broken and broken is it's own kind of beautiful"

- **Robert M. Drake**

SCARED OF LONELY

2020

30th May – one day Alcohol Free (AF)

Today is day one of me quitting alcohol. My why...well I have become way too dependent on food and drink over the last twelve months after my separation. Especially through Covid times. It's now impacting significantly on my mental and physical health and I need to make some changes. When I have a drink, it feels amazing and I am on top of the world. The day after, I feel like utter crap and fall into a major depression.

My decree nisi, following my 21–year marriage, is due on the 15th June. With the decree absolute due in six weeks and a day after that. There is no way I want to feel like this when my decree absolute is confirmed...I do not want to feel depressed and sad. I would like to feel mentally and physically strong, happy and know that better times are on their way.

I've been using food and alcohol to stop the loneliness and grief of the past twelve months. I now feel it's time to face my problems and start to learn to love myself.

I realise that for many years, all my distractions were trying to make myself complete. I was looking externally for things to fill this massive, bloody hole in the middle of my stomach, that felt empty...I know I was distracting with external things, like keeping busy, alcohol, work, food and spending money to name a few. Instead, I need to reach inwards. I also know that making this shift will impact positively on other relationships at home, in work and in friendships, as I am too often triggered by other people around me, because they are showing me things I don't like about myself.

Finding Joy Within™

I know this from working with Andy Harrington for years, that as humans, we are motivated to change because we are avoiding pain or seeking pleasure. I know that I am definitely wanting to avoid the pain of drinking right now.

5th June – seven days AF

I am now seven days AF. Whilst not being with other people, I have been totally okay. I started my AF journey last Friday and with the amount of alcohol I consumed in my holidays, I was quite glad of a break on my first AF weekend. I'm feeling proud of myself and I feel healthy. I have been digesting the videos from the Naked Mind Coaching Programme and I'm gaining more insights as to why I drink, why I want to give up drinking, why willpower doesn't work and the alcohol culture. I learn a mind changing fact...a mind changing fact that it isn't a person who is addicted, it's the substance that is addictive. Why is this? Because of the joyful feeling the first drink offers. This is such a lightbulb moment.

I am feeling okay about my Zoom party tomorrow and the prospect of not having a drink. However, I am feeling a little anxious about an outdoor gathering of five people next Saturday to celebrate our teamwork during Covid.

What I will miss is the dry, sparkling taste of the Prosecco and the instant relaxing feeling this first glass brings with it. I am also slightly apprehensive. Apprehensive about whether or not I can have as much fun without alcohol. What I won't miss is the day after, wasting the morning stuck in bed with a hangover.

I have figured out that the reasons I drink are to:

• Relax and reduce stress

• Calm my nerves

- Celebrate

- Help me get excited for a night out

- Reduce loneliness

- Fit in – it's a social thing to do!

And I do actually like the taste of a cold, glass of Prosecco. It makes me feel adult and a fun person. What if I never get that same hit, that same feeling from drinking a cold glass of Prosecco from a beautiful crystal glass ever again?

I am starting to realise that there is an element of this, which is numbing negative feelings. I am a bit scared that for the foreseeable future I will have to feel the pain of loneliness in my life, rather than avoid it.

Also, I am a bit scared that alcohol may be the only thing I had in common with people in some social situations. That I will not fit in. That friends will not like me anymore or think I'm quiet and boring. Deep down, I have no idea how I am going to have fun without alcohol and what if I don't want to try things because they just don't excite me without alcohol?

I have no idea what I will I do with my time at night. What if...????

I say to myself, "F*** this Kath, get a grip and do something to take your mind off this."

I start to research and fill my mind with positive information rather than negative what ifs.

In 2005, the National Science Foundation published an article summarising research on human thoughts per day. It was found that the average person has about 12,000 to 60,000 thoughts per day. Of those thousands of thoughts, 80% were negative and 95% were exactly the same repetitive thoughts as the day before.

We can see that one of the tendencies of the mind is to focus on the negative and 'play the same songs' over and over again.

To thrive in an increasingly complex world, we need to understand what our stories, thoughts and emotions are telling us and how they are driving us. How we manage our internal world, absolutely determines how we show up in our lives and in our relationships. We often perceive emotions as good or bad, negative or positive. However, in a world of complexity, we need to be flexible and agile with how we manage ourselves. As Susan David states, "We need greater levels of emotional agility for true resilience and thriving."

People deal with negative emotions differently; some people may wallow with self-pity and get stuck in their heads, obsessed with being right or stuck in comparititis! Others may stop perceived negative emotions, which then show up in later life when they are least expected or wanted. Neither of these ways are an effective way of dealing with negative emotions. When emotions are ignored, they become stronger. You may think you are in control if you are avoiding them, instead they control you if they aren't processed. I know this from personal experience of repressing my own emotions and from others I know repressing theirs. Many of us are aware of the foods with poor nutritional value and the impact of putting these foods into our bodies. But how aware are we of the volume of negative thoughts we are putting in our bodies that affect our cellular structure?

I know that life is about balance and we need to experience the lows to feel the highs, and I know that right now, I wish I had a lot fewer of the lows. I know that, medically, flat line means dead. Experiencing the ups and downs is part of being human and I know that difficult emotions are part of our contract with life, to have a meaningful existence and I know that right now I'm wishing for a few less.

The World Health Organisation have found that depression is the leading cause of disability globally. Outstripping cancer and cardiovascular disease and at a time where greater complexity is coming into our lives; unprecedented political, technological and economic change. This was pre–Covid. The ONS survey found that UK depression rates in adults post – COVID have doubled from 10 to 21%, with 67% of children feeling that the pandemic will impact negatively on their mental health impacted negatively on their mental health.

7th June – nine days AF

I am now two weekends AF!

I had fun on a Zoom call with my friends last night, without alcohol. Though I did leave earlier than I normally would. I felt some pangs for a drink, to feel more connected and part of the experience. I've told a few close friends that I've given up drinking, initially for 30 days. As it has become too significant in my life. They were understanding, although I don't think they fully understood why I have so much of a problem. To be honest, why would they? Outwardly, I probably appear as someone who enjoys a bit of Prosecco. No one knows the inner conflict I experience when I can't stop, the heart palpitations I wake up with at 3am and the deep depression I feel the next day, unless I know I have another glass of wine to look forward to in the evening.

I can generally cope on weekdays without alcohol, however, I've not managed many weekends without alcohol for as long as I can remember (other than while I was pregnant, in 2005!). I have tried 'Dry January' many times. I've never succeeded a full month!

Since I was 14, I have drunk. I convinced myself that the drink took away the void in the bottom of my stomach and it was my only way to have fun. The euphoric hit that I get from the first taste of cold, dry fizz at the back of my throat and the slightly sedative feeling from the first glass has been my saviour for years. I want to know how to get that feeling from somewhere else, to calm the butterflies in my stomach. At this moment in time, I've no idea where that is going to come from!

I know that trying to moderate alcohol will not work for me, as I've tried many times before and failed. I stopped drinking on weekdays a while ago. On weekends, I don't have a very good off switch! I realise that to succeed I need to change my perceptions and beliefs in my ability to live a life of joy alcohol free. I want alcohol to be small and irrelevant in my life, so that it's not the main thing I am thinking about or looking forward to at a social occasion. Two weeks ago, if someone had told me there was a get-together in Manchester, my first thought would be, right, how am I going to get there and back and how much will it cost me in a taxi so I can have a drink? If Em had asked me for a lift anywhere at the weekend, my first question would have been, what time, so that I know how it would impact on my Prosecco time! Anybody relate?

Today I had a productive day. I hired a skip on Saturday and started to sort out the loft in my house. Since we moved in twenty years ago, it has been accumulating with stuff, so much that you can't actually move in the loft anymore. Since we decided to separate in September 2019, I knew this was a task I was going to have to face. I started with the intention of healing and intentionally, without a drink! I know this is going to be a long, painful job. There are boxes in here that haven't been unpacked since 1998...from three moves ago.

9th June – eleven days AF

Today I registered my coaching and consulting business with Companies House. Something I have dreamed of for ages is owning my own business. I have two coaching clients booked who I am excited to help, so why don't I feel the excitement and pride I anticipated about starting my own business? Maybe it is because of the global pandemic situation and lockdown and that I can't celebrate with friends. Or maybe because I can't have alcohol? It felt weird not popping a bottle of champagne to celebrate. Instead, I had a lime and lemonade and watched a film with my daughter. It was nice it just wasn't the joy I was expecting to feel.

11th June – thirteen days AF

I'm really, really struggling today.

Annie Grace has been telling me, in her daily videos, that willpower acts like a muscle which can be fatigued with continued use. Thus, making it hard for people to manage addictions or behaviours with willpower alone. I know that every day that I am choosing not to drink, I am building new neural pathways. Today I am riding purely on willpower to build those new pathways.

I thought I was going to feel amazing when I stopped drinking...I don't. I stopped drinking to help me feel better and no way do I feel better. I've no idea how to have fun or experience joy without alcohol. I'm snapping at Em for no reason and I'm filled with anger, bitterness, sadness and resentment. I think it's because I feel I have been left with many of the practicalities of things to sort in the house. The loft in particular, has stirred up some stuff for me and I strongly resent the fact that I have to work so f****** hard to make positive changes in my life and my mindset. I just want it to be easy!

I know that loneliness is also a factor, as my divorce is going through court on Monday and I don't have drink to distract and numb me from all this. I'm trying to pick myself up again and know this is temporary...I am so wanting to reach for alcohol today. Instead, I decide to cry, feel and write in my journal, about all the emotions I am experiencing.

I read that it's a common thing that when you quit alcohol, you experience strong emotions which can be difficult to deal with, as previously the alcohol would just have numbed them.

I am learning painfully that my emotions are useful data. I know I don't have to listen to everything they say, but they are showing me when things are off track. And right now I don't have the tools to deal with the emotions that are showing up for me. It's 7pm and I'm off to bed... the mammoth effort of resisting alcohol to manage my emotions is too much!

20th June – twenty–two days AF

I can hear the waves lapping against the sea wall. A wave boarder is trying to ride the huge waves. The sun is setting in front of us and I am sitting with Emma in our little black Mini on Blackpool seafront. The smell of Harry Ramsden's fish and chips is filling the car and we're singing along to One Direction's 'Up All Night'. There is no way I would've done this alcohol free on a Friday a month ago. Friday and Saturdays were reserved for whatever could've been done with Prosecco and pink gin!

I feel at peace with everything that has happened and positive about opportunities that life is presenting me with. Five days ago, my decree nisi was passed through court and my loft is now cleared of things, things which were keeping me stuck in the past and that I was hanging onto.

I donated all of Emma's old baby things to charity. I kept everything in the loft in the hope that I would be pregnant again one day. It wasn't meant to be. Emma is the most wonderful daughter that I could ever wish for and I didn't want her to be an only child. I didn't want her to experience the loneliness I had as a child. These past few months have taught me that my experience is not hers. She is not lonely with her best friend Zoe living across the road and the beautiful friendship group she has at school. Emma's now fifteen and I'm forty–four. I think it's probably time to say goodbye to the sterilisers, baby grows and the guilt that I've been carrying of being unable to give Emma a brother or sister.

I sorted out childhood and family memories into boxes for Em, Glen and I to keep. As I sorted through all our things, I reflected on the happy times we had experienced as a family. I expressed sadness that we were no longer a family unit and expressed deep gratitude for the times we had spent together going on holidays, celebrating birthdays and doing the small things like feeding the ducks or going to the park. I carefully boxed up all the old photographs and family memories together for Emma when she is older, as this was a joyful part of our lives that I don't want to pretend didn't happen, even though things are different now.

Today as I sit in front of the sea, I am happy. My eyes are filled with happy tears, as I feel my life filled with joy. I am spending time with the most precious person in my life and I am proud of myself for overcoming the challenges I have faced so far. I have sorted lots of practical stuff like the divorce, the remortgage, refurbishing the house to make it my own with Em and most importantly being able to configure the Wi–Fi and connect the Sonos speaker. ☺

21ˢᵗ June – twenty–three days AF

Tonight, is my first test – a socially distanced BBQ for five people! I had my M&S zero–alcohol, sparkling Fizzero to hand. The evening was lovely. I did miss the wine a little, for about two hours, after which I felt okay and managed to relax and join in with the evening.

I am conscious though, of how I've replaced alcohol in my life with sugar. I was always so careful with food (to leave room for the wine calories!!) However, now that I've stopped drinking, any crisps, cakes, chocolate and biscuits are totally fair game. I've also reduced my amount of exercise, due to giving myself permission to be let off doing other things I find hard, whilst I am quitting alcohol. This is all fine, but I'm starting to feel an amount of discomfort around my waistline. I reckon I've added three quarters of a stone in a couple of weeks.

22ⁿᵈ June – twenty–four days AF

Today I'm blessed to be starting work with an amazing therapist, Sophia, who has developed a method to unlock back pain. I've been suffering from back pain, which I thought was caused by my posture when running. Apparently, it has been caused by disconnection to my inner child... I've heard the term before but not given it much contemplation.

According to Sophia, we all have an inner child, not a physical, little child living inside of us, or a part of the brain delegated solely to childish thought, but a part of us that reflects the child we once were in both our negative and positive aspects. Our inner child holds all of our unmet needs and suppressed childhood emotions and also holds our innocence, creativity and joy – the playful side of us.

If you ignore your inner child, it will be at your cost. That carefree aspect of you will be very difficult to access as an adult and can lead to a serious lack of joy. What your inner child knows are all the emotions to repress if you want to be loved. If you were only offered attention when 'good', you might find your inner child holds sadness or anger. If you experienced abuse, you might have learned to hide pain and fear to survive. Your inner child can also hold all of the beliefs imposed on you. For example, "You'd better not say what you really think, or else people won't like you", or "Don't try to get that promotion – you just aren't experienced enough."

In each of us there is a wounded inner child – you don't have to have experienced serious abuse, it can simply be a series of beliefs or protection mechanisms that aren't serving you. If you have experienced difficulties as a child, it can sometimes be difficult to face them and the emotions that go with them. Our subconscious mind represses our memories, but also suppresses the lighter side of us and that gut feeling that we get – our intuition.

Carl Jung, a prolific psychiatrist, described our inner child as being a way of connecting us to the past, as we recollect our childhood experiences and emotions, to then help us mature and realise what we want for our future.

Sophia sets me a task...to do fun creative things to connect with my inner child. She also suggests:

• Inner child meditations

• Learning how to soothe my inner child through journaling

• Talking to my inner child and making her feel secure (I am feeling a little skeptical at this.)

• Creating new affirmations and beliefs

I am fascinated with the science and when I'm at home I do more reading about how when we are healing our inner child, we are rarely just healing ourselves, but several generations of emotional distress and healing for generations to come. I believe there are very few parents who would ever set out to cause harm to their children, however the unhealed child inside of them causes damage to future generations. I am a little scared if I'm honest, about the damage we have already caused to Emma through the separation, I know though that if I make a commitment to heal my inner child, it should also help to pass a belief set to Em filled with hope, positivity and possibility (if it's not too late!!)

30th June – thirty days AF

I've reached thirty days alcohol–free. Go me! I've learnt much about how alcohol affects the body and the mind. I've understood more about the alcohol culture and I understand my reasons for drinking, including why I don't want to drink anymore. I didn't think getting to thirty days was going to be possible for me and to be honest it doesn't feel quite as euphoric as I thought it would. That's a trait of mine.

I managed many of the thirty days through willpower, and maybe some of my beliefs about alcohol are starting to shift. I write a letter to my future self in five years' time describing my hopes, fears and dreams for my future self, however, I don't know what my commitment to drinking or not genuinely is. I renew my subscription for the Naked Mind for another month, although I'm still unsure of my intentions.

Finding Joy Within™

"It's easy to stand in the crowd but it takes courage to stand alone"

- **Mahatma Gandhi**

HIGHER LOVE

7th July – thirty–eight days AF

Tonight is difficult... I am distracted by scrolling through my phone and eating crap... I know alcohol was solving a lack of inner connection problem for me and I've no idea how to try and get the inner connection without alcohol. I'm a meditation teacher and even meditation isn't working. I'm scrolling Facebook and WhatsApp looking for connections, which isn't helping. I just can't focus and decide to take myself off to bed at 8.30pm. I'm reaching a place of acceptance where I just need to ride these emotional waves, however, they are still occurring more often than I would like them to be!

14th July – forty–three days AF

My life is continuing to expand with beautiful people and experiences. Here I am, sitting in my hot tub with Emma in the sunshine. Café del Mar music playing in the background, pretending we're in Ibiza. One of things on my vision board was to have a hot tub in my garden.

As an Aquarian (don't hold that against me), I have always had a love for water. Being around any kind of water, be it the sea, a swimming pool or a lake, brings me deep relaxation. I think I probably get that from my dad too, who is a keen fisherman. No holiday is ever complete for me without a boat trip! When we holiday with our friends, Andre and Simone, they know we always need to carve out a day for a boat trip. ☺

My garden was one of my first real manifestation experiences from my vision board. When I started to redesign the interior of my house last year, I drew the picture of my ideal garden and put it out to the universe and on my vision board. This week, it delivered for me. Given Covid, it's probably the closest I'm likely to experience the holiday vibe this year. My cancelled holidays have enabled me to invest in my home and garden and I am truly grateful.

I've had to do a lot of re–patterning since the tub was installed at the beginning of July, as when I ordered it, I was planning to use it to host parties whilst drinking champagne. Now I am envisioning an entirely different purpose of peace, rest, rejuvenation and serenity, although at the moment, it doesn't seem quite as exciting!

16th July – forty–five days AF and my first 'data point' (what my coaching group call it, each time you have a drink in your AF journey)

After forty–four days free of alcohol, at my friend's BBQ yesterday, I caved … I had a bottle of AF wine and an AF beer, it was just not hitting it for me. Then, I thought, maybe just one?

I drank two glasses of Prosecco alternating with other non–alcoholic drinks and stopped. This morning I woke up having not slept well, although I didn't have a hangover.

The fizz was very easy to drink and I was deeply mindful about drinking slowly and mixing with AF drinks. It made me realise how much and how quickly I must've drunk previously.

How do I feel about it? I don't feel shame or that I've let myself down. Drinking felt familiar, though my alternating was a different experience. The conversation was nice and I had fun. I'm aware that I do still have a deep held belief that, if I'm not drinking, I'm depriving myself.

Finding Joy Within™

I felt in control of my alcohol consumption and decided today that if I choose to have the occasional drink as a treat, I can be in control. However, I'm not sure if this is a cop out.

Without alcohol, I feel deprived and put more sugar into my body, which impacts my weight and my mood.

I spend some time reflecting on how alcohol has added and taken away from each of the positive emotional states as described by American psychology professor, Barbara Fredrickson:

• Love – Alcohol helps me to relax and express myself at the time, though sometimes I do feel remorseful in the morning that I might have over–shared and been over– emotional.

• Joy – Alcohol makes me feel more adult, more joyful, more worthy. I have realised that a glass in my hand of anything reduces anxiety, though with alcohol in it the anxiety levels drop much quicker! However, alcohol keeps me stuck in an old pattern, searching for something else or comparing.

• Gratitude – When I've had wine, I express drunk gratitude, which is very gushing. I prefer real, sober gratitude. I also sometimes forget my gratitude list in the evening when I've had a drink, which I don't like, for reasons I've expressed before.

• Serenity – I might think I look serene at the time of drinking wine, however, often I look awful in photos when I look through sober eyes.

• Interest – I'm more confident to ask questions with Prosecco, though they may not always be intelligent ones, and may be repetitive or gossipy.

• Hope – I've hope whilst the drink is there, although it's temporary. I also have hope without alcohol, however, that's temporary too.

Finding Joy Within™

• Pride – the same experience as with hope. Drinking excessively fills me with shame and potential embarrassment the day after, depending how much I had. Interestingly, moderate drinking didn't fill me with shame as I could remember everything and it didn't make me unwell.

• Amusement – It's easier to laugh, including at myself, with alcohol. I don't think I'm a naturally fun or humorous person and alcohol helps me with that. However, alcohol makes me depressed and anxious the following day and less able to connect with my inner child, who I actually need to connect with to have fun!

• Inspiration – I feel inspired when we are planning alcohol-infused night. When the morning comes, I might not even remember all of the night! Without alcohol, I have inspired ideas that light me up, however alcohol steals my creativity!

• Awe – I feel in awe of many people when I've had a drink, I'm not sure I would always feel the same awe when sober?

After these reflections, I have committed myself to:

• 3 AF periods: New Year until my birthday, 1st June until 10th July and 1st October until 10th November

• No drinking at home on my own – always an AF alternative

• 4 blow outs per year – I will plan to be unproductive the day after

• 2 nights of drinking per month with 3 drinks per night permitted, with the exception of holidays. This is my personal treat.

• Holidays – need an AF day every other day

• I will drive where I can, to reduce costs of nights out, unless it's a special treat

Finding Joy Within™

I want to be able to do long stints of my life without alcohol, I don't feel like I want to say I'm completely AF, as I think it's too much pressure for me. I want to be able to say I only drink on special occasions and actually mean it. Part of the reason I drank at the weekend was the fear that I could never be fully in control if I never tried alcohol again. For me, if I hadn't drunk again after I had given up, I would've always been wondering if I could moderate. I have proved to myself that I can on one occasion. Not sure what's next...

What I didn't realise at the time when I wrote this list, was that I was making my decision and making my fatigue worse by setting parameters around alcohol. The more decisions we have to make, the more difficult it is to make wise choices. By not making a firm decision not to drink, I was leaving myself wide open to decision fatigue, which is exactly what happened next.

18th July – no longer counting AF days...

I'm having a bit of a wobble today. I am feeling distinctly alone and not sure how to self-soothe. I feel like I should be proud of myself, as I have run two marathons in the Lake District over four days, taking me about 16.5 hours, but I'm not. I registered for this event with Vicki, my running buddy. I enrolled for an additional weekend distraction to avoid drinking as I know I never want to risk training with a hangover. I felt greatly proud of myself exploring new routes on day one when I ran 22 miles around Ullswater lake on my own. I met up with friends in the Lakes and decided to have a couple of drinks to celebrate my achievements, not imagining the damage it was going to do after having got alcohol out of my system. I enjoyed the night, had a laugh and celebrated my achievement. However, on day two I walked very slowly four miles, when I should have ran ten, as I felt sick and rough all day which affected my running for the rest of the week.

I think I'm going to have an early night and hopefully wake up feeling sunnier in the morning. I demolished a massive bag of salt and vinegar crisps, telling myself I needed salt … but I did avoid alcohol to soothe or celebrate. I'm conscious I've committed to only drinking two nights a month and I've used these up already.

I know I've put my body through a huge challenge and succeeded and there will be a low. I'm missing not having someone to cheer me on, I also know it's an opportunity to get to know and motivate myself.

I know my body and mind need some real self–love for the next few days.

27th July

I am struggling to come to terms with my divorce and the fact that I'm seeing pictures of my ex (sorry – The Ex) with his new girlfriend on holiday, on good old Facebook! I'm trying to put a brave face on it, however, my body is carrying so much tension. I know wine would relax it and I'm desperately resisting opening the bottle. Right now there is nothing else I can think to turn to. Again, I try to meditate; it's not cutting it, so it's off to bed for me again at 8.00pm!

28th July

5am – Well, I didn't drink which is positive. This morning things just feel pointless and tiring. I don't know how to shake my way out of this.

I know that my irrational, worrying thoughts are just that, but the pain they cause is so familiar. I'm feeling intensely jealous of

Glen's relationship. I'm really missing physical contact and I'm struggling to keep my confidence and optimism levels high.

I'm struggling motivating myself this morning, even though I have a couple of hours before I start work ... I am really frustrated with myself that I can't control my anxiety levels and decide I'm going to spend an hour outside in the garden. I've found recently that nature has a profound impact on soothing my soul.

I feel inspired to pray! Where did that come from?

My spirituality has always been important to me in my life. I went to church with my grandparents when I was little, helping them to clean the brasses inside the church. It was important to me that I was married in a church and that Christianity was part of Emma's school life. I've always had a desire to develop my spirituality and developed a Buddhist practice for a couple of years alongside my Christian faith.

During my separation, and at various times during my marriage when I was struggling, I turned to God to help me, although only when I was in trouble. Putting my faith in something bigger than myself was not a routine part of my life when things were going well. As part of my healing process, I started to connect with people and groups to help me grow spiritually. I also followed the Twelve Steps (Alcoholics Anonymous) AA programme at the start of the year. Many people believe that the Twelve Steps programme is only for alcohol and drug addiction, in fact it's relevant for every addiction and at the time (I was telling myself) that mine was negative thinking.

I say the Lord's Prayer and ask God to guide me on what to do next.

I feel the words channel through my pen to me as I write...

Kath,

My will for you is that you can make yourself whole and complete. You are doing amazingly, you need to work this through on your own so that you are 100% accepting of yourself.

You don't need someone to tell you that you are kind, caring, beautiful and amazing. You know that, I know that, your friends know that and your daughter knows that. You need to believe and feel it. Fill the emptiness with the belief in yourself and your faith in me.

I know that you want a partner to help you through trials and difficulties. You need to trust in me and trust in yourself, before you trust in anyone else. You have great things to teach others, you need to be whole yourself to help others.

Put your faith in me. I will ensure that you always have everything that you need. Put your faith in me for new decisions and live your life as frugally as you can moving forwards. Writing has to be a priority. Put your faith in me that together we will get your book written by the end of August. You need to prioritise writing every single day. Don't feel stuck with this, you are a brilliant writer. Use the creativity you are using now to journal in your book. You have so much to share to help other people know, trust and love themselves.

I know you may be doubting yourself and how you heal from this loneliness. Connecting with you, me and people that uplift you is the only way to make you strong. Everybody who you need in your life to make you whole is in it now, you don't need to search for anyone. Find and appreciate the diamonds in your life now.

What has happened with Glen has happened. Be grateful for Emma, for a second chance at life for both of you and don't waste your energy in the past. When it comes to others, don't compare.

Finding Joy Within™

Remember, you are entering into one of the last few summers with Emma as a teenager, spend time with her, have fun with her and focus on what you want your life to be like. Your new routines, your business, your work, things you are going to do together, things you are going to do on your own and things you are going to do with your friends.

Your new habits need to be fun and things that inspire you – start learning to dance – you need to do this as it will give you so much confidence and joy. Stick to keeping your body toned and strong.

I promise you, I have your back. You will have a partner in the future who will fill you with joy and happiness, however, you need to be whole, complete and fulfilled by yourself first.

Love God x

Whilst writing, I started to cry. I've got to be honest, I questioned where on earth all of that came from and if it was just me talking to myself. I choose to believe it came from a higher power than me.

16th August – the start of taking alcohol out of my life again

I feel like I've let myself down a bit. I did a 43 day AF stint June into July, but then drank on four days in July and five days in August (three of those in the past three days).

My triggers were, not feeling like I could do social things without alcohol and needing to socialise for the past three days, because Em was away with her dad, his new girlfriend and her children. I decided I wasn't going to be on my own. I also knew I wouldn't have the strength to say no to alcohol. I had a lovely weekend spending time with friends, however, the majority of activities involved alcohol and I probably had the equivalent of three bottles of wine over the three days.

The result today:

• I feel tired, depressed and have little motivation to do anything

• I didn't even think about non–alcoholic alternatives at any point, which shows me I can't moderate

• I know I will feel the real sadness five days post alcohol. This is a pattern I've noticed following my drinking.

• I'm irritated about what I have spent

Based on the good things that have worked for me over the past three months, I have planned my new morning routine to put in place at the same time as quitting alcohol again:

• Prayer

• Affirmations

• Meditation for positivity

• Visualisation

• Exercise

• Getting ready for the day as if I were going into the office – it's become a bit of a challenge to keep work and home separate post Covid

Now to be earnest, I've no idea how to pray alone. However, with the help of the internet I've found a couple of prayers to start with.

At night I'm going to focus on reading, getting my book finished, relaxing in my hot tub and walking the dogs with friends.

My potential rewards are a spa day, new clothes or make–up, a spin bike or a rebounder. Not decided yet.

My stick is giving my daughter £100 each time I drink, although I'm not going to tell her that! ☺

I've decided not to drink for a minimum of thirty days, maybe ninety, with the intention of proving to myself that I can have fun without alcohol.

Now I'm just trying to decide if I should start today or two weeks from today. I'm going camping for a week next Sunday and I'm not too sure I'm ready for that without alcohol. The advice from Sandra and Robbie (the Naked Mind coaches) is to do big things without alcohol straight away. Robbie advises, "If you give yourself an option, leave the door open, you will probably drink at camping." Hmm, food for thought.

17th August

I'm waiting for Emma to return home from her holiday and there's a knock at the door. A brown envelope sent 'recorded delivery'. I'm quite excited as to what it might be. As I open it, the excitement quickly disappears and I'm not sure what the feeling is – uncertainty, fear and sadness. Also mixed with a small glimmer of hope, possibility and optimism. It's my decree absolute. I am officially divorced on the day my daughter is returning from her first holiday with a different family unit. Thanks universe! At least it's closure.

As is mandatory for any problem these days, I turn to Google and ask for 'ways in which to mark a divorce'. I'm struck by how many of the suggestions I've already done: take up exercise or a new hobby, take a holiday, see a therapist, develop a vision for your life, sort your finances, create your house as you would like and clear out your cupboards. I'm surprised at how many involve alcohol, (a bit of a problem for me right now) and how many I perceive as quite negative behaviour or focusing on the past: burning your marriage certificate, wedding dress and photos, selling your wedding ring and buying something your ex would hate. The ideas I did embrace:

• Planning something fun to do with friends (once Manchester is out of lockdown!)

• Planning a holiday with Emma (whenever I can get on a plane)

• Getting some professional pictures done with Emma

• Connecting more strongly with the vision for my life and the actions I am going to take to move towards it.

There was an interesting idea about having a "we're divorced party" with your ex, bridesmaids and groomsmen. Gotta be honest, I'm not healed enough for that. Nor am I ready for plastic surgery for whichever part of you your husband would be envious about, or moving a new man into my house ... LOL.

Google hasn't been a huge help to me in this situation and I know the answers are within me. I need to trust in God, my guides and myself.

Finding Joy Within™

After my new–found connection with prayer, I have more wisdom and inspiration from praying. My latest advice from God:

1. Find inner peace and make this your new normal. Ditch the drama! You are going to get things thrown at you every single week and you need to be as grounded as the tallest tree in the woods.

2. Develop your mental, physical and spiritual strength. You need to reprogramme the muscles in your body and brain.

3. Find ways to have fun without alcohol and prove to yourself that they are just as much fun without the booze! Look at your list of things you want to do, how you want to be and what you want to have. Prioritise your time and relationships, so that you can do some of these things.

4. Look at what you're talking about. Stop the conversations about the past and negative conversations. Focus on the future and find a new way of living in abundance. Connect with the people and networks that will support you in your quest to be happy.

5. Finish your book – this is something you can be proud of and will also help other people in this world too.

6. Forgive, forgive, and forgive. Let everything go with love in your past. Holding onto hurt is not serving you – it's hurting you and not hurting them. Learn how to see everybody through the eyes of compassion. Even those who have hurt you. Holding onto negativity and resentment will only keep you from your quest of inner peace.

Love God x

I am now working on getting myself into a positive place to make sure I don't just bombard Em with lots of questions when she is back this afternoon from her holiday.

Finding Joy Within™

26th August

So I lasted two whole days on a camping holiday, without drinking, which was a major achievement! We were with friends and had a lovely time without alcohol initially – canoeing on Ullswater, leisurely walks, pub drinks and picnics by the lake. I've got to be honest, in the sunshine with friends and everyone else drinking, I was white knuckling some of this, overall though I had a wonderful time! This gave me hope. ☺

Unfortunately, we got rained away on day three in our motorhome and decided to return home early yesterday. Spontaneously (very unlike me!) we went back with a different tent last night. I was proud I'd pitched the tent on my own and Prosecco with friends was my reward. I had a glass but I couldn't stop at one and then had the bottle. As you can predict, I feel like crap today.

Today I had a glass of gin at the pub and a glass of Prosecco. I enjoyed it so much and should've stopped, but I couldn't. I went and bought a bottle of Prosecco to take back to the campsite. I had one glass from the bottle and felt such disappointment with myself that I poured the rest of the bottle away; what a waste!! I'm now determined I am going to do 100 days AF – no negotiation.

"Think about it, there must be higher love. Down in the heart or hidden in the stars above. Without it, life is a wasted time. Look inside your heart, I'll look inside mine"

- Steve Winwood

RISE UP

27th August – Day 1 again... My last day one

After drinking on holiday, I know that moderation is just not possible for me. I can't say no and once I start, I don't have a very effective off switch.

I know I have to make some firm commitments to myself to not drink, to continue to immerse myself in re–educating myself about alcohol and use the support from the Naked Mind Programme.

For the past two months I haven't focused much on increasing my knowledge about alcohol and its effects and it shows by my 'data points'. Naked Mind Material Day 1 : The Power of the Unconscious. Research has shown that we make our decisions seven seconds before we are consciously aware of making them. To gain control of our decisions and our lives we must make the unconscious...conscious. I realise I have to dig deeper into myself to uncover more of my beliefs.

My whole life I have felt lonely and judged. On reflection, I know these thoughts were a mirror of how I was feeling in myself rather than by anyone else. When I was married, I didn't want to drink alone in the house as Glen wasn't a big drinker and I felt he may be judging me, so I constantly arranged for us, as a family, to be out in places where I could drink – this caused many time pressures and got us into debt.

What I now realise, is that I probably wasn't arranging to go out just to socialise. It was because I wanted to be sociable, it also permitted me to drink, to dull my state and to numb the internal pain.

I'm ashamed to say this, I think my beliefs about alcohol being fun stem from the fact that I would think someone was boring if they didn't drink. The reality of it was, if I was with someone who didn't drink, the night would likely end earlier and I would have to go back to my internal pain of loneliness and judgement. I was judging them as boring. Actually it was because they were reducing the time I could spend distracting from pain

So where am I now? Well, I can see something I've not seen before. Now I am on my own, I feel less judged and sometimes a little less lonely, as I can be still with myself. I am starting to love and accept myself and put my faith into something bigger, I now need to work on building joyful experiences into my life.

I am surprised by what I am learning about how alcohol affects our bodies' balance physically. About how much alcohol increases the amount of dopamine in our brain (the pleasure hormone) from the first glass and how by the fourth or fifth has a negative impact on your feel–good hormones. I am starting to understand why I get such a hit from the first glass that isn't replicated after that and why I have found it so difficult to replicate that initial euphoric feeling. After one drink we experience a massive rush of pleasure, however, after a few drinks we have put our bodies into a state of stress with alcohol, that the body has to work hard to reverse.

6th September – Day 11 AF

It's Emma's birthday on Wednesday! I can't believe she is 15 already. I remember the day she was born like it was yesterday. I loved being pregnant and the moment she came into this world was the happiest day of my life. I had never felt love like it when I looked into her eyes. I spent the whole night in the hospital staring at her and the same on the first night we brought her home. I feel a little sad today at the fact that Glen and I are not together any more, as I think we were a happy family during the time that we were together. I don't think either of us had ever felt such love and pride like we did on the day she was born.

Right, wiping the tears away... Back to my alcohol dilemmas... We are having our amazing support bubble over for tea in the garden tonight. It's the first time I'm entertaining in my new garden and the first time I haven't had some sort of big celebration for Emma's birthday! Our friends, the Leadbeaters, live across the road from us. I have known Ian pretty much all my life through the brass band, and his wife, Claire is now one of my besties! We both had our girls at the same time and Emma and Zoe have grown up like sisters – every time I see them together my heart bursts with the love that they have for each other.

Anna, their younger daughter and my Goddaughter is such a beautiful soul too – we talk lots about spiritual stuff! ☺ I love them all dearly and I am looking forward to them coming over, however, I've got some anxieties about my first family birthday celebration without alcohol. Simone jokes that any birthday, (even my dog's – I kid you not!) was an excuse for a party at ours. It was! It was also an excuse for me to drink. It's a beautiful day and I put my alcohol–free cider in the fridge to help me through the evening.

To help with my distractions and to have some fun, we play pass the parcel and musical chairs – Em is mortified at first...the kids soon get into it as well! ☺ I actually enjoy my first birthday celebration AF and I'm feeling proud of myself. Go me! I'm going to bed with a clear head, the kitchen clean and everything prepared for work tomorrow. I had a nice time and didn't miss the alcohol – my first big win!

9th September – Day 14 AF

It's Emma's birthday today and we can go to restaurants! That's a big thing for us in Bolton, having had restaurants shut for what feels like forever! I take Em to a local restaurant and I drive. This is definitely my first birthday celebration driving and I really like it. I asked the waitress to make me an AF cocktail and I feel supremely proud of myself! We had a lovely evening together. ☺

11th September – Day 16 AF

I don't want to drink but I want this sadness to go away. Being on my own, I just feel so lonely this weekend and I want it to stop but don't know how to! My friends' suggestions are that I get on a dating website. I don't want to do that for many reasons, including I don't want to date whilst I'm trying to go AF, plus I don't have the time. I'm questioning why I'm trying to improve my body and my mind if it's not to be healthy in another relationship...

Kath – remember, it's to be healthy with yourself. You need to show someone else how you expect to be loved.

But I am really missing physical connection. I remember the research that I shared in my Tedx talk about the importance of 12 hugs a day to thrive. I am barely getting the 4 to survive at the moment, as I suspect many aren't due to the pandemic.

12th September – Day 17 AF

As I prepare to spend the day in the garden in the sunshine, I come across the scan of Peanut attached to the back of my sunglasses case. Peanut was Emma's baby brother or sister. Unfortunately, it wasn't meant to be. Peanut was on and off from week 6 until week 16, when unfortunately he (I think it was a he) wasn't strong enough to survive inside me and I had to say goodbye.

I thought that another child would complete me. I now know there is only me who can do that. I think that was my theory on our two dogs as well, if I'm honest with myself! I showed Em the picture of my scan – she said, "aww that's really sad" and gave me a hug. I said I know, it wasn't meant to be – 'we' were meant to be.

25th September – 30 days AF

One of the most lovely things happened to me tonight. I was chatting to my friend Dena and was telling her I didn't know how to mark my 30 days AF without a drink! Being an expert in play therapy she organised a surprise Zoom quiz and got some friends from the Why's Council to come. I was so touched by her thought and the fact that people took the time to share my success with me, even though I don't know where this journey is taking me. I've completed 30 days. I don't know what's next. Ninety days and even 50 days seem impossible. I've used willpower to get me through the first 30 days. How am I going to get through holidays, my birthday and Christmas without alcohol? This 30 days feels different though. In June, it was almost like 'Dry January' (which I had always failed...). I was looking at it as a time limited thing, so there was always the possibility of alcohol at the end. Now I am taking that option away, and it feels scary.

My internal reminder – Kath focus on the now and take one day at a time.

30th September – 35 days AF

Today I am a published author! I have contributed to a book with my friend, Lisa King, and fourteen other authors sharing their stories of overcoming adversity, with proceeds going to an incredible charity supporting the mental health of people that are feeling desperate and suicidal – Megan's Space.

Whilst my chapter isn't solely focused on alcohol, my interview to support the book launch interestingly turned out to be!

After a few weeks of my prayer and meditation practice, I can feel a huge shift in the connection I have with myself and the universe. The hole in my stomach doesn't feel nearly as big and I can tell now when things aren't flowing easily that I'm taking Kath-guided action that is all driven by head-based decision and action, rather than, spiritually-guided action that is all driven by heart and intuition decision and action. It feels difficult, hard work and pressured when it's Kath-guided actions that are guiding things. I know I need to keep my morning and evening rituals in place to keep me connected to my inner child and something bigger than myself. This is a bit of a challenge at the moment with the busy nature of life. However, I'm persevering...

11th October – 46 days AF

I'm feeling sad tonight and not sure why. I've had a stressful week at work this week, with the same planned for next week. My diary is back–to–back with team meetings. I know I'm lacking serious joy in my life and struggling to find activities to do with my Em to lift my mood, especially when it's pouring down with rain ... I won't pick up a drink, even though I feel like it would just give me a lift ...

As I dig more into my emotions I start to understand more fully why I'm feeling like this and come to a better place of acceptance:

1. I've been doing some coursework today for my therapy course and it's all about the inner child. I've had to dig deep into some shit, which has affected me. I'm not feeling very authentic about coaching people to live their best life when I feel I'm not living mine this week.

2. Working in the health service, the prospect of gearing up again for wave two of Covid isn't motivating me. I can't give it the energy I did last time because I just don't have it in me.

3. My daughter's boyfriend Alex, who's lovely, was over yesterday and I guess signaled a change in her to me, about her growing up. She doesn't see it. I feel very melancholic. The song from Mamma Mia 'Schoolbag in Hand' goes round in my mind and I shed a couple of tears.

4. Looking at Facebook this evening (still not managed to break that habit) and seeing everyone's fun, family pictures on a Saturday night, mine feels a far cry from that. I'm feeling quite envious (not proud to say that) – I think I'm going to find the Covid situation harder to cope with in the winter than in the summer due to being on my own. I know that people's lives rarely look the way they do in the photos we share online. Sometimes I fall too easily back into the comparison trap again.

5. I have invested a great deal of time, love, energy and money into my home to make it my sanctuary, which it now is. However a lot of the time it feels calm. Calm to me = boring. I have some work to do on this. When I dig further, I come to realise, that when I was younger I know I calculated silence = anxiety.

I know that many childhood experiences show up in our older years in fears and anxieties and there is some stuff here that I still need to address. I know fear should be reserved for bears in the woods, but however, my brain sometimes doesn't know the difference between what's real and what's imagined! I know my anxieties are worries about things that might never happen, yet they still sometimes take hold of me.

Someone in my alcohol–coaching group asked me today, what does peace mean for me. Peace is having the butterflies in my tummy go away. Interestingly, if you had asked me that one to two years ago I would've said, to fill the void in my stomach. It's not actually to do with the external environment I've realised.

Trying to move myself positively forwards, with the help of Google,I start to dream of the things I want to do and know about myself in my life. So here goes, with my bucket list for the future. ☺

1. Salsa dance in a Manchester bar

2. Party and dance through the night – no alcohol!

3. Spread out a map, point and just go there

4. Go to a music festival

5. Row a boat on a river

6. Pick a date for my trademark party and have one every year

7. Go back to Ibiza

8. Take Em to Disneyland in Florida

9. Watch the sunrise from a mountain and set over the sea

10. Swim with dolphins

11. Go on safari

12. Book a spontaneous holiday

13. Go canoeing

14. Go to a comedy club

15. Experience a treetop adventure park

16. Read Hitchhiker's Guide to the Galaxy

17. Buy a stranger a drink

18. Go to a summer solstice on a sacred site

19. Have a spa day

20. Go abroad on a spiritual retreat

21. Stand under a natural waterfall

22. Climb a tree

23. Sunbathe naked

24. Visit a temple not of my religion

25. Volunteer more

26. Go to Lourdes

27. Go to a food and flower market abroad

28. Go back to Jamaica

29. Read in nature for a day

30. Visit a botanic garden

31. Learn to summersault / handstand again

32. Go to the opera or ballet

33. Own something that I feel is really beautiful – a piece of art

34. Ride my bike again

35. Tell my friends what I admire about each of them

36. Do something creative under a full moon

37. Help someone who is unhappy

38. Binge watch Netflix

39. Go paddle boarding

40. Go to a theme park

41. Have a campfire and toast marshmallows

42. Visit the Maldives

43. Play adult Twister

44. Plan a luxurious picnic for people I love

45. Get dressed up and go to an extravagant restaurant

46. Go somewhere I don't want to with an open mind

47. Sit outside and daydream for a day once a month

48. Lie on my back in a forest and listen to the trees

49. Meet some of the people who have inspired my personal development journey

50. Go to a Tony Robbins event

And things I would like to find out about myself:

1. My happiest memories that will make me smile when I'm sad

2. Things that soothe me when I'm stressed

3. Five new places I want to visit

4. My favourite dance

5. My favourite smells

6. My life motto

7. My favourite animal

8. My family history

9. My favourite actor

10. The actor I want to play me in the movie of my life

11. What I take for granted

12. The landscape that speaks to my soul

13. My biggest regret and figuring how I can make up for it

14. My 7 sins and 7 virtues

15. My favourite song

16. Skills I would like to learn

17. The saddest thing I've seen and why

18. My 12 signature dishes from 12 different countries

19. Describing to a child of 5 what I do for a job (I think that may be my biggest challenge...)

20. People/places/activities/things that inspire me

21. My favourite memories as a child: books, toys, food. people, games and where I played as a child

22. Name 10 people I love and make sure they know it

23. Listing my 5 most important values, 5 key strengths and 5 weaknesses

24. The most romantic vacation I would like to experience

25. Who would I swap a day in the life of and why?

Finding Joy Within™

13th October – 48 days AF

I feel blessed to have been part of a panel for Mental Health Awareness Day today in one of my personal development groups. Focusing on this topic, I greatly fear for how our health and care services will cope in the aftermath of this pandemic with the mental health issues the whole experience has caused for our population. I know, I need to keep my vibe high, so I went for a two–mile run and enjoyed a coffee in my hot tub. I am feeling blessed today – I am focusing on what I want to attract into my life and learning to not let my fears live rent–free in my head.

14th October – 49 days AF

One off my bucket list today! I went paddle boarding with the Bee Sober Bolton group and really enjoyed it! I loved the peace and tranquility I felt in the middle of the lake on my own. I also had real fun and giggles with the games we played as a group. I chatted to people who have been alcohol–free for way longer than I have and I felt hope that it was possible to create a life of joy without alcohol.

"As long as there is life, there is a potential; and as long as there is a potential, there will be a success! You will sprout again when cut down! You will rise again even when you fall!"

- Israelmore Ayivor

AIN'T GIVING UP

15th October – 50 days AF

I've been struggling with sugar cravings and reduced motivation to exercise, since I decided to cut myself some slack in this area of my life when I quit alcohol... I started to work with a fitness coach, Adam, a couple of weeks ago, to help me get my food and exercise routines back to some form of normal.

I am 50 days alcohol–free which is the longest period of time I've not drunk since I was 15, other than when I was pregnant.

My stress levels have been increasing massively this week and my connection to technology constant, as I'm sure is the same for many now working remotely. I was starting to feel anxious last night about my holiday next week and being around alcohol. I was deeply questioning myself how I was going to resist, given my failure on day three of the August holiday.

This morning I trained at the gym and then have been on teams all day. I was still thinking about the alcohol challenge and getting anxious – that word again – about another deadline I had missed...to get the first draft of this book to my publisher.

This book has been two years in the writing and it's never felt complete enough to write. All I could think about by 2.00pm was a bottle of wine, a cupcake – no idea why that – and living my life in deprivation.

I looked at my food plan and realised the meal I was due, I could swap for a protein bar. I've now come to view protein bars rather than chocolate as my treat! Once I realised I could have something I view as a treat, I actually didn't want it and understood it was something else my body needed. So I went to lie down for ten minutes with a glass of water. I'm wondering how many times something as simple as this may have stopped me drinking or consuming many calories? This was a big learning experience for me.

There is a technique which is used in my alcohol coaching group for the times that you get a craving for anything. You are encouraged to ask yourself, "Are you hungry, angry, lonely or tired?" I had forgotten all about this until today and it worked!

17th October – 52 days alcohol–free

I'm riding the emotion wave again this morning.

I'm using my hangover–free time in the evenings and weekends to work on my book. I am proud of myself for my 52 days alcohol–free, however, the urge hasn't passed yet to drink Prosecco in social situations and I'm anxious about my forthcoming, tee–total, holiday situation next week.

I had a very disrupted night's sleep last night. My little dog, Hope, started choking about midnight before I went to bed. I spoke to the vet who told me to just observe her. I was worried about Hope, so she slept with me and it was like having a baby in the room again, with very little sleep,

Additionally, I'm riding the loneliness wave this weekend. Being solely responsible for financing and looking after the house, being a mum and a leader, feeling bad that I've missed the deadline to get my book finished, having sole responsibility for my parents as an only child and not having anyone to share stuff with is making me feel really f****** sad. The victim inside me is properly coming out to play. I don't have an urge to drink, I'm just a bit tired of all the hard work. I'm just wondering when I will start to feel happier about this process.

I looked at my weight and body photos from six weeks ago, when I started my new nutrition and exercise programme and I can see only a little change in physique and only 1kg of weight loss as a result of what I've changed in terms of food types. I would've expected more impact than that and was feeling a bit pissed off with myself until Adam, my coach, started to educate me on the impact of stress on potentially reducing weight loss. I need to remind myself that what I eat today will have a strong impact on how good I feel tomorrow! And that constantly living in a state of stress and anxiety is not helping my weight loss at all.

I'm constantly checking my phone at the moment looking for connection. I'm scrolling aimlessly, getting few positives and many negatives from it, so I'm aiming to have a tech–free week next week whilst I'm away. I'm acutely aware that I need a week ahead which is light–hearted!

After a recommendation from a friend, I started to read a book on compound interest, which is about how our efforts over time compound and then "suddenly", after struggling, we start receiving a reward for our investments. I'm hoping this applies to me too! The Compound Effect by Darren Hardy is based on a principle that little everyday decisions that you take will either, take you to the life you desire, or keep you stuck or on a downward trajectory.

Rather than focusing on the negatives of my situation, I write:

• 50 reasons why I am grateful for being single

• 50 reasons why I am grateful for my family unit as it is

• 50 reasons why I am grateful for not drinking

• 50 reasons why I am grateful for not drinking on holiday to try and lift my mood

I feel marginally better...

20th October – 55 days AF

So, I made it through the first night of the holiday! I craved Prosecco for the first hour or so, especially in the excitement of being on holiday, then I didn't...and this morning I am doing my mediations and journaling, hangover–free!

24th October – 59 days AF

OK, so I am back from my first holiday alcohol–free. Yay!!

There were some enjoyable things:

• Waking up hangover–free

• Waking up remembering everything about the day before

• Knowing that the enjoyment I had was true enjoyment and not the relaxation of inhibitions due to alcohol

• Pride of not breaking my AF streak – I am on day 60 tomorrow!

• Intentionally having fun and finding other activities to re–pattern my belief that being AF is boring. I cooked, walked, danced and went horse riding. I've never ridden a horse before (other than the donkeys on Blackpool Pleasure Beach with my Mum and Dad). The loss of control was a major trigger for me. Once I was content with that, I found myself enjoying trotting through Sherwood Forest on a horse ☺

There were some not so enjoyable things:

• The smell of wine was driving me mad for the first hour every day when people were drinking and I was desperately craving alcohol. I know that for the first hour I miss it and it's an effort. After that it's okay. Hopefully this time will get shorter the longer I am AF!

Finding Joy Within™

• I was craving that dry and relaxing hit of alcohol that I wasn't getting from AF drinks

• I lost some of my 'why' – other than reaching the 100 days and again started to contemplate if I can moderate...I know that's a slippery slope.

This week I was definitely reliant on willpower, rather than mindset shift. I am proud of myself, but it was an emotionally tiring few days. I am an introvert so exerting this much energy to not be boring has left me feeling so drained. I need to recharge my batteries before I go back to work on Monday.

26th October – 61 days AF

Two days after arriving home from holiday and maybe it wasn't just my extroversion that was making me tired! I've been diagnosed with Covid–19 and I feel like shit! I know that the basic things that keep me grounded and well went to the wall a bit pre–holiday with the business of life and work. Things I had done on holiday have taken some effort – the nutrition, the not drinking and even fun stuff, as it's not my natural state of being!

I am absolutely exhausted and I physically can't get out of bed.

14th November – I don't care about AF days anymore!

Two days ago was my first day out of the house after contracting Covid and was the first day I've been out of bed for more than half an hour. I've had to ask for help, (which does not come easy to me) looking after Emma and walking the dogs, as I've been so exhausted. Fortunately, my lovely friend Sue and her children have been taking the dogs out for me. I am so grateful to them.

Yesterday I was feeling the effects of my first period of exertion. After my short walk, my hands and ankles swelled up like when I was nine months pregnant. My heart rate was 150 beats per minute after a 0.2 mile walk and I felt like I had run a marathon. I had a dreadful, drowning feeling through the night and the swelling got worse. After ringing 111, I ended up in hospital, with the conclusion that my heart and lungs were okay, and that I may be one of the cases where Covid symptoms from a muscular and cardiac/chest perspective are taking longer to recover. Great!

The last 24 hours in hospital has forced me to admit how much the Covid lockdown stuff; working hard, not asking for help and changing my eating and drinking habits has impacted on my mental and physical health. I know I'm going to need a couple more weeks off work as I physically cannot work. I feel so guilty knowing how much pressure my team are under to support the health care system during this pandemic.

"Life is like riding a bicycle. To keep your balance, you must keep moving"

- Albert Einstein

HEAL

22nd November

As I prepare to go back to work next week, I'm trying to build my strength back up slowly. I've been for a lovely walk today. It was only for thirty minutes and for a short distance, however, I'm finding that nature and the trees are having a very healing impact on my soul.

Tonight, I had a lovely bath. I'm finding new things to nourish my soul and support my healing journey, both mental and physical.

I had an interesting day today. I had a therapy session with Sophia and we were looking at my disconnect from positive emotions. After developing Covid, my mental health has deteriorated even further and I need to try and get some positive perspective back. The doctor in A&E had suggested maybe going back on antidepressants... I really didn't want to do that. After coming off them at the end of 2018, that wasn't a place I wanted to go again.

Sophia asked me to complete a map of my life in five-year blocks, with key memories, events, people and beliefs in each – my goodness that was depressing and traumatic. I was physically sick and cried so much. I realised that I was feeling grief. I hadn't grieved for anything properly in my life – being lonely as a child, my marriage, my miscarriage and parts of my life that had been consumed by alcohol.

I was also aware of the negative memories outweighing the positive memories throughout my life, especially when I was younger. I found there were many photos I could not look at because of how much I disliked myself. My conclusion, with Sophia, was that I have some major inner healing to do and so I plan to spend more time each day praying, meditating and sending love to my younger self.

I know I need to move forwards positively, establish a routine, let go of the past and focus on the future.

I am going to start to:

• Ask my guides for help

• Ask people for help (I am rubbish at this...)

• Believe in myself, my affirmations

• Live in joy and gratitude and prioritise the things I want to do each day

• Read and listen to positive videos and books, because they help me live in a world of possibilities

• Cleanse my mind, body and spirit

• Say no to things (this doesn't come easy to me as I'm a people pleaser and I don't want to upset people)

• Do creative writing

• Spend quality time with my dogs – I have seen them too much as a burden since the separation

• Pray

I am going to stop:

• Distracting and procrastinating

• Talking about the past

• Living in fear

• Thinking of everyone else before me

• Self sabotaging

• Comparing myself

Finding Joy Within™

I am going to continue:

• Prioritising time with Em

• Working on myself and moving forwards

• Meditating

• Moving a little each day

• Making alcohol small and insignificant in my life, knowing I can be joyful without it

25th November

I've walked for a short distance every day for three days to try and build my strength up for work, although I think I've done too much. I'm physically exhausted and as much as I don't want to admit this, I'm going to have to listen to my body and go at the pace it is allowing, rather than me trying to push the process.

I've spoken to a couple of people in the past 24 hours about my Covid recovery and my journey with alcohol. I do believe the two are related, as I think I may not have gotten so run down had my immune system not been so compromised. Firstly, by the stress of the separation and secondly, by the stress associated with not drinking. I no longer have an easy release valve or a way of dealing with the wave of emotions.

I'm due back into work in a couple of days and my anxiety is building, given how much energy I lack, I've been off for five weeks now, including my holiday and I'm feeling really guilty that I'm letting my colleagues down.

26th November

I know that many of my younger years were lost because of alcohol and behaving older than my years. I now need to fully live my life without alcohol.

After spending a couple of days regularly meditating and praying I'm feeling my heart starting to open. This morning I admired the brightest sunset I have seen in ages through my window.

I need to stay connected to God and my inner child and listen. I know I won't need acceptance from others, or feel pressure anymore to do things that aren't good for me, if I listen to my inner guide. The guilt and shame I've been giving my inner child for years is not what I would be putting on Emma and I need to treat myself kindly.

My task for this week is to go with the flow, genuinely feel gratitude and focus on the successes in my life. I've bought myself a Brag book to fill each day with three things I am proud of about myself. I feel quite sick at this prospect if I'm honest!

27th November

Today, I bought and built a trampoline rebounder! It's apparently very good for boosting your lymphatic system, losing weight and reducing stress! I've put it in my spare room with my meditation chair and I'm going to try a combination of bouncing and meditation to start my day when I return to work on Monday.

I am a bit anxious about going back to work, and worried I'm going to end up in the same cycle of stress as before my holidays. I'm not tempted to drink wine, although I do want to eat chocolate to soothe my anxiety. I know it's because I've not figured out how to make my inner child feel safe, secure and loved right now ... I will keep trying and not cave into the chocolate.

28th November

It's my weekly Naked Mind Coaching call and my alcohol coaching group are asking me "what are you going to do Kath to celebrate 100 days AF? What are you going to do about drinking after that milestone?" I said I would "celebrate by getting my hair done, (assuming the hairdressers are still open), going somewhere nice to eat with friends and driving home."

The problem is, I still don't feel a huge amount of excitement saying I am 100 days AF. Even though, I do feel pride. I say I'm still not sure of my post–100–day plan, though I know the safe way is to not go back to drinking alcohol. It just feels like the hard way at the moment...I'm trying to balance hard work vs just going with the flow and seeing what happens. I don't think that going with the flow is the right approach.

I'm still struggling with sugar and snacking since I caught Covid, which I need to sort. I'm not feeling connected to 'my why' for not drinking and 'my why' for not eating crap. Though, I did see an old video of me skiing today, where I was half cut and overweight a couple of years ago...and that was some motivation...

Christmas has been causing me great anxiety for a variety of reasons and the prospect of experiencing it without alcohol, quite honestly, is f****** scary. I hold a fundamental belief that my Christmas will be miserable without alcohol and I need to try and reframe that.

Using a technique that I have learned on my alcohol coaching course, I try to reprocess:

Finding Joy Within™

My current belief

I will be miserable without alcohol. Everyone else will be drinking. It will reduce my anxieties, help me feel more relaxed and help me to connect better with people. I love the taste and I'm craving that crisp taste of fizz at the back of my throat. My Christmas experience will be incomplete without alcohol.

My new understanding

I am choosing not to drink for the following reasons:

I want to be hangover and depression free the day after. Especially as I won't be with Emma on Boxing Day.

I don't want the impact of the calories from the alcohol and what I might eat as a consequence.

It's not enjoyable after the first one or two drinks, by then it has taken hold and I can't say no.

Not drinking is helping to build my confidence about making positive changes in my life. It is giving me a sense of confidence and achievement.

I can drink if I want to, I am choosing not to.

I miss out on what my body is telling me when I am drunk.

I don't want to be wondering what I said, or what I have done with important items such as a my phone, my keys or my purse!

I want to experience true joy in my life, without numbing pain or looking to a bottle to find joy.

I am role modelling positive behaviour to Em.

I am saving money on alcohol and taxis by not drinking.

I can still be and have fun without alcohol.

I can drink whatever and whenever I want, any day. I am choosing it not to be today. I feel a little nervous, a bit excited and happy that I have chosen to be alcohol–free.

My commitment

I commit to not drinking over Christmas.

I will be more present for people because I am focusing on them and not the bottle.

I will do lovely fun things that I remember and have the freedom to leave and drive to other places if I am not enjoying myself.

I won't be wasting money on taxis.

I will feel good about myself and know that I am developing knowledge, skills and experience to help me and others to lead more joyful and faith–filled lives.

This all said, I am approaching day 100 now AF. I do have an element of fear and curiosity as to whether or not I still even like the taste and the impact and I desperately want the answer to be no. I feel too scared to try.

I'm not sure of the best way of overcoming this fear as I'm now seeing alcohol as something I'm phobic of, which I'm not sure is a good thing either.

After weighing up the pros and cons, praying and meditating, I've decided today that I'm not going to drink again for the foreseeable future. Whilst I find this a little exciting, I'm experiencing intense grief, however, it's what I need to do.

I cried so much when I came to this decision and for some unbeknown reason, felt I had to write a goodbye letter to alcohol!

Dear Alcohol,

I want to thank you for what you gave me in my life since I was a young teenager. You gave me, on a temporary basis, a way of distraction. You gave me a way of feeling connected and fitting in when I was feeling lonely, a way of feeling safety and a way of feeling positive emotions and excitement.

As I got older, you turned into a habit that I could not break and every weekend I was socialising to drink. If this didn't happen, I felt like I was missing out. I thought it was missing out on the people, actually it was probably missing out on the highs of alcohol just as much. What you brought me was a huge amount of debt, because I always had to be out of the house socialising and drinking, as I never felt comfortable drinking in the house socially. Drinking in pubs and restaurants was fair game.

There were times, a few years ago, when you gave me good company in the house after everyone had gone to bed, when I was working late. If I hadn't opened a bottle of you, I probably wouldn't have been able to keep going until 1am with my work! When Emma was young, you were the thing that got me through the four hours of work every night after I had put her to bed. After Glen and I separated, you got me through the deep despair of loneliness and heartbreak.

There have been times I have done things I am not proud of – invariably they have involved you and some 'Dutch courage' at the start. I should have listened to my gut and inner child, that these were not the right things to do – I have learned from that now.

Looking back on my life now, I actually realise that drinking in pubs from such an early age put me at some risk. On reflection it has also brought me a great deal of shame that I didn't recognise. I realise now, looking back at old photographs, that I remember actual events in time and space when a fun event happened and alcohol was involved, I don't remember the detail, which makes me sad. What I noticed also from my photographs, is that there were many events and moments of joy I didn't remember (probably because the high wasn't as big!), though the experience of the events was just as positive.

There have been many occasions where I knew that drink was a problem I didn't want to admit it:

• I was terrified at the prospect of not being able to drink when I got pregnant.

• I've struggled with nutrition plans that needed me to ditch alcohol.

• I've never been able to be the 'designated driver' or drive to social events because I could not face the prospect of not drinking – this has contributed to keeping my local cab company going!.

• I've never been able to stop at one drink. I have to finish the bottle.

• I've been ashamed to look at photos or videos, or hear stories of what I was doing the night before, when I know I've had a lot to drink.

Finding Joy Within™

You gave me great solace from loneliness when my marriage broke up, especially as I no longer had to worry about drinking in the house alone and you were my new–found freedom! However, my turning point to stop was seeing the ten green bottles on the sink in May.

The ironic thing is that I'd been going to a Christian Life Recovery group doing the 12 Steps programme, to free myself from addictive negative thinking. In all that time, sitting at the weekly meetings, never once did I ever confess I had a drinking problem, as I didn't think I had, compared to other people. I was holding my life together. I wasn't wanting to drink during the day and I hadn't turned to spirits, therefore I must be okay. Instead, I had been distracting and denying myself finding unintoxicated, real joy in my life.

I watched Bad Moms this week and viewed the Christmas celebrations with envy, where they were partaking in alcohol and having fun. I felt grief that I may not experience that high again, I also know that I will not face the lows. I'm also living in hope that, as my confidence without alcohol increases, I can have as much fun without alcohol in that sort of social environment, as I once could with alcohol.

In line with my normal mental patterns, I've only remembered what I'm interpreting as my failure days when I did drink since June and not the 93% that were positive changes towards finding my joy within. I would not have believed this was possible if you had told me this 12 months ago. The good things I have experienced so far include:

1. Pride at breaking a bad habit.

2. Being proud to be different and having something new to talk about!

Finding Joy Within™

3. Trying new things – I wouldn't have gone paddle boarding and I wouldn't have been insistent on filling my days with good things to do on holiday AF. I wouldn't have the support I have of friends through the Naked Mind programme and Bee Sober group.

4. Being able to have as much fun without alcohol (after the settling–in period).

5. My eyes look more sparkling, my skin is clearer and I no longer have hangovers!

6. Saving money and having freedom to drive to new places without worrying about where I've put my keys, phone or purse and the taxi bill home.

7. Creating a home I love and I am connected to.

8. Not worrying about what time Emma needs a lift in case it interferes with my wine time!

9. Driving to Blackpool with Em for fish and chips on a Friday night just because we could.

10. Doing my 50 mile virtual run – it was a distraction from alcohol with the training!

11. Going back to our camping holiday with our tent as we were washed out once! Previously I would have stayed at home drinking. Unfortunately, I did go back camping and drink …

12. Starting my nutrition plan, something I could not have contemplated six months ago, as I couldn't have coped without alcohol. I can see some small changes in my physique.

13. Trying new drinks and alternatives I may never have considered before, the variety is amazing, especially with the help of my friend Lisa's NonToxicated! app.

14. Finding new things to fill my time with; TV, films, books and music that I've never given myself permission to enjoy before.

15. Participating in manifestation challenges which have delivered me my car, my garden and a new Ted Baker dress! I would've been too focused on alcohol to give these things the time.

16. My Find Your Why 30–day AF party

17. Getting my breakthrough. I've only been able to do this as a result of Covid stopping me in my tracks. I owe it to my inner child and God, to stay on the right path now and listen to what my body is telling me.

18. I have learned some skills that may help others to change.

Alcohol, it is now time to let you go. You have served your purpose in helping me have a good time when I was younger. However, the day–after effects of depression and illness, and the lack of joy and true connection with people are not worth it.

I know I may face some resistance for the first hour of any social event, but I also know that the benefits the day after will be worth it. I will remember the whole night, I won't feel shame looking at videos and photos of the night before and I will experience deeper joy and connection with those around me.

I owe this to my inner child who has dealt with so much guilt and shame as a result of drinking alcohol to give her confidence. She has been left damaged and feeling unsafe at times. Now, I need to love her with all my heart.

I don't regret anything in my life concerning you, as it's taught me what I want to do with my life and how I want to live my best life. However, I now need to make some positive changes to help others and myself.

Finding Joy Within™

Thank you alcohol and goodbye.

Kath X

Until I made this decision, I was still holding onto part of my old world, whilst trying to transition to a new one. I hope and pray that this decision will free me to be the person I want to become, rather than clinging onto my past.

29th November

I was feeling high levels of anxiety about going back to work and my energy levels were still quite low. So I decided that I wasn't joining in with our weekly Zoom quiz last night, which is very rare for me and I received some lovely support from my friends:

• Sue delivered pizza for my tea, and offered to walk the dogs if I needed help during my first week back.

• Vicky brought brownies from my Goddaughter, Ellie. Ellie is such a talented entrepreneur who has started an amazing cake business – Ellie's Cake Creations! I'm so inspired by her passion, her talent and her creativity.

• Clive dropped off some lovely flowers for me, from him and Natalie.

• The Leadbeaters invited Em and me for tea tonight

• Simone rang me for a chat.

When we returned home from the Leadbeaters, Em said to me, "Mum, you really do have lovely friends don't you? I don't think my friends would make this much effort if I said I wasn't going somewhere because I was feeling a bit down!"

I go to bed feeling very lucky and blessed to have such amazing friends in my life (which I do already know ☺)

30th November

My alarm goes off at 6.30am. As soon as I wake, I feel sick at the prospect of my day ahead. I took myself off to bed at 9pm last night to prepare for my first day back at work, I know my body isn't prepared. I force myself through the process of getting ready, the school run, and logging onto Teams.

I haven't looked at a computer screen since the end of October and as I see myself on screen I'm horrified at what I look like and the glare of the screen isn't helping my vision post–Covid. Twenty–five minutes into the meeting and I can't actually remember what Lindsey said to me fifteen minutes earlier. I know I haven't got the energy to manage the demands of my job. I barely have the energy to manage holding back the tears, never mind anything else.

As I hang up from the call, I sob hard for two hours. I know I'm not ready to go back to work. I'm worried I'll never work again if my cognitive functioning doesn't come back. I speak to my friend who is a GP, who counsels me that my thinking is probably a bit extreme, given it has only been five weeks since I contracted Covid and only three weeks ago that I was hospitalised. I try and put some perspective in my life, even though again I feel consumed with guilt that I still can't go back to work. I also feel really angry. I'm angry at myself for not being able to get my health back on track. I'm angry at myself for not being able to control my emotions and detach from my marriage. I'm angry at myself for not making better financial decisions and I'm angry at everyone else for not seeing my pain.

2nd December

I watched a Diana documentary tonight and it upset me deeply. I think the whole relationship dynamic with the press, the sadness in her life and seeing her two boys at the funeral, having to deal with that grief so publicly, really hit my heart. I'm finding without alcohol I'm so much more emotional and can cry at the drop of a hat, whereas previously, I would've kept it all bottled up. I think I'm maybe now feeling many previously dulled emotions that are now coming up.

I've no idea why I watched it or why I have this strong, uneasy feeling afterwards, but I do... Maybe about a wasted life of someone who wanted to do the right thing and was so insecure about herself.

I'm losing faith today. The further anxiety of what has gone on at work is taking its toll in terms of my mental state. I'm worried and my worries start spiralling...I might not be able to work again because I rely on mental cognition so much, then I might not be able to afford the house, then we might have to sell the house and then...and then...

I say to myself..."Kath – STOP AND BREATHE".

I feel I need to just press a stop button right now and rebuild everything in my life. I feel like I have all the Lego pieces on the floor in front of me and need to build it back with only the things that are serving me.

Most of all, I know I need to be patient and that this will happen in God's time, not mine. I have to quit with the forcing and the pushing – it's what I've done all my life, I know it's not going to help when it comes to my health, especially when I've spoken with the GP about how to manage long Covid.

My friend Liz, who suffers from fibromyalgia, teaches me a technique to see how much energy I have each day, then only plan what I'm going to do on that day according to how much energy I have. This seems alien and almost impossible for me, when I generally have my life planned out weeks in advance, I realise that all I can do is take this illness one day at a time.

I know that I need to practice letting things unfold, rather than trying to fix them and letting people help me - this all feels so weird. I also commit to staying off social media (which, to be honest with myself, I've not really been on since I contracted Covid) and to finding the habits I need to keep me well.

"You have the power to heal your life, and you need to know that. We think so often that we are helpless, but we're not. We always have the power of our minds...Claim and consciously use your power."

- **Louise L. Hay**

TITANIUM

2020

4th December

100 days alcohol–free! It's a bit underwhelming because I'm still feeling like crap post Covid. Nonetheless, I am feeling proud of myself. I didn't think this day would've been possible six months ago

I have celebrated by buying a new drinks cabinet to fill with fabulous alcohol–free alternatives!! I am grateful for all the support I have had on this journey from my friends, family and in my coaching group. This has been a rollercoaster over the past six months, and I am glad that I started the journey. I finally decided today, that this year will be an alcohol–free Christmas for me. I feel a sense of relief and a sense of dread.

5th December

Today the universe was definitely testing whether I meant I wasn't drinking this year or not... universe really!?!?

Glen has just collected Em and told me he is moving in with his girlfriend next week. Now my daughter and my dogs are going to have to go and integrate with a new family arrangement. I'm absolutely devastated. This was my absolute worst nightmare following the separation.

As he leaves the house, I go to the garage and get a bottle of Prosecco to open. It's 11am. I sit in my kitchen, the foil peeled off the cap and I'm about to pop the cork when I gain some clarity and realise this will help nobody, least of all me. I pick my keys up and drive.

I drive and drive and come across a church car park where I pull in – I have no idea where I am. I go and sit on the church steps and ask God why the f*** is he giving me more stuff to deal with – I can't handle any more!

I sob for a couple of hours and then reach out to friends who are able to help me process my feelings and know that I am not alone. It feels like a different world to yesterday. Yesterday I was so determined. Today, I'm so helpless and everything feels hopeless. I know that self–compassion, patience and self–love will see me through to the other side of this and not alcohol...man it's hard. Why do I keep getting these curve balls?? What more do I need to learn??

It's the evening and I'm off to my friend's with my AF wine. I'm so glad I'm allowed a support bubble! Interestingly she didn't drink. I was the one who needed to hold something that felt like wine to soothe me. I stayed for a couple of hours and then came home. The old me would've not been stopping at two and a half hours – I would've been properly hammering the wine through the night as it stopped the mental pain and torture for a while. I'm slowly finding ways to soothe myself. In the moment, it can still feel like I'm standing on burning hot coals in difficult situations.

6th December

I am glad I didn't compromise my 100 days AF by reacting to someone else's decisions. I feel like Bambi – I keep trying to stand, but keep falling over and don't know how to stabilise myself properly. Especially as I'm feeling under the weather.

I know I am creating a completely different life for myself that will be better than it was before. One of my friends pointed out to me that Bambi grew into a beautiful deer – I like that analogy, although I don't like the fact that he got shot!

18th December

It's my daughter's first weekend with her dad, in his new home, with his new family. To make it worse, it is his 50th birthday, which is making me feel slightly melancholic. I'm feeling vulnerable and my catastrophic thinking about every aspect of my life is kicking in, where I always assume the worse case scenario and turn little problems into big ones. Sometimes, I think I anticipate issues so much, that I can actually create them! I feel the pain, so that I know nobody else can make me feel worse than I do about myself ... WTF is that about?

All of our brains are wired to survival, however for me, a fundamental belief growing up was that the world is dangerous, making my brain programme itself to keep looking for danger. This viewpoint has sometimes served me well to manage risk, not so much as a human.

In my life I've been in a holding pattern that if I assume the worst, I'll feel less shit if something bad actually does happen. I'm trying hard to change this, as this mindset means I can't live a happy, balanced and joyful life. I know I have to take a different approach and commit to these things:

• Moving

• Getting into nature

• Writing

• Taking to friends rather than isolating myself

• Going with the flow and feeling what my body needs

Finding Joy Within™

120

20th December

Putting these things into place whilst Em is away for a couple of days is helping me to ground myself.

This year, we have all been forced to spend a great deal of time in our homes and I know it's not just where you live that's important...it's getting outside in nature too. Being in nature, has been one of the biggest healers in life for me over recent months. Being in nature or viewing nature, can result in a marked reduction in emotions. In a recent study by Mind, 95% of those interviewed said their mood improved after spending time outdoors. By focusing on nature and something more than ourselves, it provides respite for our busy minds.

I was struck by one of the members of my nursing team, who during Covid, described the positive impact that just leaving the ward and feeling the fresh air on her face had on changing her mood. Many of us take these things for granted, so easily.

For me, being by the sea always energises me and is a big part of why I love summer holidays so much and why I've missed them so much this year!

26th December: My Christmas blog...

So, it was 120 days alcohol–free for me on Christmas Eve and as you already know, I had made a conscious decision I was not going to drink over Christmas a couple of weeks ago.

When we were allowed, over Christmas, Em and I saw friends and relatives. A couple of friends came round for food and drinks. This was the first time I had hosted anything at my home since the separation, partly because of Covid and partly because I haven't felt like I've wanted to. It is certainly the first thing I have hosted with our support bubble, AF, with the exception of Em's birthday get–together. I made a conscious effort to make the house look nice and to make myself feel good.

I went to the hairdressers on Christmas Eve and got my hair curled. I painted my nails, Emma did my makeup for me and showed me some new beauty tips. ☺ I debated putting my jeans on or a red dress for Christmas Day, which I bought last year and didn't feel confident in before now. Now I feel good, due to the small amount of weight I've dropped, plus the inner strength I've developed. I decided to go for the red dress to make me feel special and celebrate! Celebrate the weight I'd dropped, feeling much healthier, my improved inner confidence and feeling more comfortable with my body, without the extra alcohol and sugar weight and lasting after effects.

I was not fully wedded (pardon the pun) to staying in the house when we separated. However, it was important to Em that we stayed in our family home and I was in the fortunate position to be able to afford it on my own by making some sacrifices. Since the separation, I've totally re–energised the house by decorating, changing furniture, adding artwork and putting in energy remedies to align with the feng shui of the house. As you know, I also have my beautiful garden sanctuary!

As I waited for my guests to arrive I opened my sparkling tea (my Xmas drink treat to myself from Fortnum and Mason) and poured myself a glass. It was surprisingly nice and felt like Prosecco. I didn't feel like I was missing out.

Time together with friends was lovely and I didn't really miss alcohol. I made a delicious buffet, we played some games and had giggles. Everyone said what a lovely time they had had. For the first time in my life, I felt I had been a successful homemaker, which has not been such a big part of my life before. As Glen worked from home, he ended up doing lots of the household tasks, because it was logistically easier for him. Looking back, this may have contributed to some of our issues. Whilst I was really grateful for his support, perhaps I took him for granted. I think it took away some of my joy in doing simple things, which I'm now starting to find again and may also have taken some joy from his life too. I remember some of these small joys from when we had our first house together and I'm starting to find them again.

We played Christmas carols on our street on Christmas Day, as the pubs weren't open for our usual carolling event. It was fun and I think brought a bit of joy to the neighbours!

At 10pm on Christmas Day, I took my dogs out for a walk for an hour. In previous years by this time, I would've been straight in bed after too many sherries. As I walked back indoors, I realised that this would be my first sober Christmas in 31 years. When I was pregnant with Em, I was five weeks' pregnant at Christmas. I didn't find out I was pregnant until the 3rd January, so I didn't even have a sober Christmas then!

I don't feel any anxiety about the rest of the festive period anymore. The only three things I now have to experience without alcohol are, my birthday in February, any big gatherings such as a wedding and an all-inclusive holiday abroad – hopefully in August to Turkey!

I'm looking forward to today reflecting, relaxing and reading as Em is with her dad for the day. Having survived my first experience of being alone whilst Em was at Glen's new home, the prospect of this is not such a major trigger of anxiety and panic for me anymore.

I know that this will all be okay – it's only a couple of days and I'm happy for Em that she is going with her dad to see my nephews today, who she's not seen for fifteen months since we separated. Although it does seem weird that I'm not part of that family dynamic anymore.

Finding Joy Within™

31ˢᵗ December

I have previously hated New Year, and all the expectation to have a good time and make resolutions. My grandma, who I was close to, died at New Year and I was expecting my second child on New Year's Eve and instead had to have a surgical termination at 16 weeks because the pregnancy wasn't viable (as you know). This year is different. My New Year's Eve was lovely and I enjoyed the day immensely. I went for a walk in the snow in Rivington with Simone, who we normally ski with at New Year. She brought me an alcohol–free beer for New Year's Eve to celebrate! Simone has been so kind and considerate towards me through this whole experience since I separated.

I got a bit emotional early evening, facing grief about so many things, I changed my evening outlook with a bath, a cup of coffee, did a short meditation and took a short nap to make me feel better.

I then spent the evening with a bottle of sparking tea, Em and the Leadbeaters (who I wouldn't have survived lockdown without!) We played some games and had some fun. I bought a couple of the fake gins and vodkas for cocktails at midnight. I actually think I am past the need for fake spirits now (which is a win, as they're often as expensive as the real thing! ☺) The rest of the evening I was just as happy with my grenadine and lemonade!

"You shoot me down, but I won't fall I am titanium."

- **David Guetta**

THIS GIRL IS ON FIRE

2021

1st January – My Year!

I woke up a bit tired as we went to bed at about 3am. I am hangover free and know that I have done something good for my body, mind and spirit this year already. It didn't feel like an effort at all not drinking – it is now just what I do.

My focus for 2021 will be on continuing my healing journey, getting my strength back after developing long Covid and finding joy without alcohol in my life.

I am planning to go back to work in two weeks, so I will need to take extra care to manage my energy levels and balance work, rest and play in my life. I'm looking forward to this with hope and optimism.

As Einstein says, "Insanity is doing the same thing over and over again and expecting different results." As I start to rebuild my life, some fundamental beliefs and rituals I know need to continue to shift. I've made a start and I know the universe has my back.

I've been working with Sophia to determine my '5 non–negotiables' to support my own self–care, which I need to get more clarity on. My intentions for the new year are to move for thirty minutes a day, to meditate and pray for thirty minutes a day and to do something that makes me smile for thirty minutes a day.

I realised last night that part of the reason I hate New Year so much, is that I have this expectation of myself. This expectation of myself is that on New Year's Day, when I wake up, I will be a much better person overnight. I won't have any negative thoughts, I won't be triggered and all my positive habits will be in place...I mean how totally unrealistic is that expectation of myself!

I think I am in a place today where I know it's about taking the small steps, putting the building blocks in place and enjoying the journey wherever the path takes me.

Tonight I found myself burning my old bed in a fire pit, at the Leadbeaters. Letting go of the past and things that are no longer serving me. On every piece of wood that I burned, I wrote something that I was letting go of and it was very therapeutic!! Fear, sadness, loneliness, anxiety, comparison, goodbye ... I burnt a lot of wood ! ☺

My wins in 2020

• Catching Covid – it forced me to stop, be present, be grateful and re–evaluate my life to build it on firmer foundations, which are not dependent on other people and things. The challenge for me will be making sure I keep these building blocks in place when I go back to work and making sure I don't go back to old ways. I have reconnected with myself and with my faith and I will not let this go. I now appreciate the simple things much more than I ever did and understand the negative thought patterns that hold me back.

• Quitting alcohol, rebasing relationships and learning to feel into rather than reject my emotions.

• Finding new ways of having fun and connection in a world of Covid!

• Learning to ask for help – I had no option when I caught Covid.

• Navigating a divorce process and now being divorced, owning and running my home. This is the first time I have run a home independently, as I was married when I was 21.

• Accepting the fact that Glen has moved in with his girlfriend and that Em is integrating into a different family unit. I didn't think I could cope with this, until Boxing Day when Glen collected Em and I realised that I felt very little emotion. Two months prior, I would've felt devastation.

• Redesigning my home and my garden (including my hot tub).

• Becoming a co– author in Stories of Truth and Triumph Book 1 by Lisa King.

• Running a couple of webinars on leading joyfully and Finding Joy Within.

• Becoming a published TEDx speaker and speaking at a couple of live/ virtual events earlier in the year.

2021 for me is about:

• Building on what I have started to put in place this year.

• Prioritising my own health when I go back to work and making sure every day I prioritise the following things: my health, my mindset, meditation, spiritual connection, movement and doing something I love each day.

• Spending quality time with Em and my friends – I am hoping we may get to travel abroad at least once this year.

• Being a good leader at work.

• Publishing my own book by the spring.

• Learning to dance – something I've always wanted to do.

Looking after Emma and myself, enjoying my life and enjoying my work are my priority right now.

This year I am saying yes to raising my vibration and will start each day with these affirmations:

I am filled with joy, happiness, optimism, gratitude, love, inspiration, aliveness, faith, peace and hope.

I have freedom in my life and have a healthy balance of work, rest and play.

I am enjoying the journey of my life and creating magic every day.

I am focused on my health, my connection with my inner child and my connection with God to heal myself and to nourish my relationships.

My self care routine:

Morning (40 mins)

• Prayers and 10 minute meditation

• 20 minutes mindset listening

• 6 minute diary – gratitude, intention setting and affirmations

• 3–5 minutes rebounding

• Cup of tea or coffee

• Not looking at my phone until I have been up for an hour

Daytime or evening

• 30 minutes of movement 5 days a week

• 30 minutes of something that brings me joy every day

Throughout day

• Water

• Vitamins

• Nutrition according to macros

Before bed

• 6 minute diary (happiest moments, wins and how I've helped someone)

• Evening prayers (stop; sorry, thank you, helping others, offering my problems)

• Not looking at my phone for at least 30 minutes before I go to bed

• 8 hours sleep

Fully getting into nature at least once a week and outdoors for a walk 4–5 times a week, depending on when I have the dogs.

6th January

Now if you read my list and thought – oh my, that sounds exhausting and hard work, well it was! It was draining holding myself to that much pressure and rigidity.

So here goes with my 5 simpler non –negotiables:

1. Start the day with a STOP prayer (sorry, thanks, helping others and helping me with my priorities prayer) and a daily bible reading to help me stay connected with God

2. Move for 30 minutes each day

3. Connect to my inner child each day. I know she loves dancing, singing, baking, being outdoors on her terms (especially in the sunshine!), being in water and being childlike

4. Early morning empowerment. Weekends: no plans before midday. Reflection and connection time and time to do whatever

I want. Weekdays: Get up in time to make myself look nice and be in my office in time to ground myself.

5. Finishing each day with my 6 minute diary and intention setting for the following day

Other givens: 8 hours sleep, good nutrition, vitamins, water and being alcohol–free.

11th January

Here I am again – my first day back at work. I'm a little anxious given my previous experience of returning to work post–Covid, last November. I feel like I'm a different person coming back with new knowledge about the importance of my health. This whole experience has taught me that without my health I have nothing and only I am responsible for my own well–being. After day one, I feel more relaxed and believe that this will be okay, as long as I keep my focus on the right things, including my mindset. I am truly grateful to all my team and colleagues for how much they have supported me whilst I have been off with Covid.

23rd January

Today I am celebrating 150 days of being alcohol–free!

My post to the Naked Mind Coaching Programme and (gulp) my Facebook page:

"As you may know, during lockdown 1.0, I decided I was drinking too much for the wrong reasons (loneliness, grief and stress), and in June joined the Naked Mind Programme and decided to give up alcohol for 30 days. If I'm honest, I got through this pretty much on willpower alone, but it was the longest period of time I had not drunk in almost 30 years (other than when I was pregnant).

After my initial 30 days, I had a few data points in the summer, as I didn't have a plan for my sobriety, and in August decided I was going to aim for 90 days alcohol–free. This felt like an impossible scary challenge when I committed to it, as I knew willpower alone wasn't going to get me through major events such as birthdays and holidays, where alcohol had previously been a key part. I really had to double down on how I changed my beliefs about alcohol and how it added to or detracted from the good things in my life.

After I broke the back of 90 days, I committed to experiencing my first Christmas in decades alcohol–free – gotta be honest that was scarier than 90 days! I did however enjoy my first Christmas alcohol–free with my sparkling tea, and am still on this path of exploring life without alcohol.

I am not saying I will never drink again, but right now I am happy experiencing all the emotions as they arise, feeling them, riding them, and waking up the next day hangover–free. For too long I had used alcohol to numb sadness, and to experience happiness. I am now rediscovering how to find pure joy in the small and simple things in life.

I am happy that through one of the most challenging times of my life, which included getting divorced in 2020 after a 22 year marriage, working as director in the health service through Covid, home schooling my 15 year old daughter and contracting and recovering from long Covid myself, I have remained alcohol–free

Finding Joy Within™

and have kept a positive focus on my nutrition, and my mindset. Yes I have down days, but I am just learning how to sit with the discomfort and find new ways to soothe myself.

I am truly grateful for all the support I have had from my friends, The Naked Mind and my Pathfinder Coaching group whilst I have been on this journey."

So far, I have kept my alcohol journey fairly private but decided I would share on Facebook. I got 166 likes, my most popular post ever as I'm not a big social media user! Lots of people telling me they were proud of me (which was nice, and I'm proud of me ☺), but most importantly it started connections with people who I had not seen or spoken to in ages, some of whom were exploring similar things with alcohol.

Brooke, the daughter of my friends Mark and Mel, is one of the most inspirational people I know. She posted me a lovely comment saying:

"Whenever I'm struggling I look up to you and think, what would Kath do, and this always gets me through."

This comment along with others, meant so much to me, and started me thinking that maybe I should be more confident about sharing more of my journey and strategies that have helped me through the difficult times?

"It took me quite a long time to develop a voice, and now that I have it, I am not going to be silent."

- **Madeleine Albright**

MAKE YOUR OWN KIND OF MUSIC

2021

5th February

It's my 45th birthday next Wednesday. Last year, six months after my marriage breakdown, I spent almost ten days with friends and drinking alcohol with the excuse of 'celebrating'. I now recognise it as 'distracting'.

Last night I celebrated my birthday with friends on Zoom at an online cocktail party.

I was quite anxious/excited at the thought of not drinking. How I was going to experience it, what it was going to be like, etc? But I wanted to arrange something fun for my birthday. I was aware of a butterfly sensation in my stomach that would not go away all day. In reality, I know it's been there for months. (I think because of general uncertainty and chaos in the world too.) Today it's been more heightened. I opened a bottle of alcohol–free Prosecco, whilst getting ready. Whilst holding the glass and tasting the fizz did make me feel better, the sweetness rather than the dryness of the taste and absence of toxins in the drink didn't take the feeling away. I knew that it wouldn't... I took time to enjoy getting ready instead.

I know this feeling well and I know that when I am feeling a bit wobbly, alcohol turns this uncertain feeling into confidence or relaxation. It doesn't do it quickly, hence why I used to drink a couple of glasses very quickly to get that feeling of stability as soon as possible. I now know this is a very false sense of stability...

As the party started, I did feel very slightly envious due to my lack of alcohol, whilst also extremely grateful I would be waking up with a clear head in the morning and I would remember everything!

I made myself some lovely cocktails — some purely juices and sodas and some, which used AF replacements. I learnt some stuff too. ☺

Finding my path to joy, although I am experiencing lots of positives, isn't always an easy or quick route. I know for certain that numbing my feelings with alcohol won't help — it will take me back into my comfort zone.

I know this is about riding the emotional wave when it appears and looking for the next best emotion I can reach for, to take me one step closer to the feeling of pure joy that I am looking for.

I have learnt that when I have identified an emotion, I have a decision to make as to whether or not I sit with an emotion as part of a healing process, or whether or not I need to make a change. I have learnt through my grieving process in November that there are times I need to sit and accept negative emotions. However, I also know that if I am regularly in a pity party for one, having a tool to change my state has been invaluable!

I have spent five days (obviously virtually!!) with Tony Robbins recently at the New World | New You Challenge and have learnt loads about energy and how to get into "peak state". The key to changing your emotional state is changing your physiology. Tony describes emotions as action signals, which can be changed by the way we perceive things (how we are seeing things) and by the procedures we run (the things we do based on our information).

I'm finding it easier to change my state, by being clear on what I want and doing something which moves me closer to the direction of what I want. When I have negative emotions, I have learned to see them as a trigger to determine what it is I need.

I've been listening to Tony's interpretation of the messages each of the emotions are giving us.

Uncomfortable	You have to change your state, get clear on what you want and take action towards it.
Fear	You may need to change the perception and not the procedure. You may just need to accept that you need to focus on things working, rather than things not working.
Hurt	Evaluate if there is a loss or if you need to change your behaviours to prevent this feeling in the future.
Anger	Somebody else, or you, has violated an important rule you have. How we deal with this will determine how effective our relationships are, e.g. if we expect things of people and don't tell them. You need to communicate in a different way or change your rules.
Frustration	You need to change your approach to achieving your goals.

Disappointment	You need to realise an expectation/outcome that you are after is unlikely to happen. You need to come up with a more appropriate outcome.
Guilt / regret	Guilt serves you if you hear the message – it tells you that you've violated your own standards. Some people may deny the guilt, or surrender to the guilt and feel so regretful that it ruins their life. The purpose of guilt is to make sure you learn from your mistakes and change your actions or your perceptions in the future. Apologising to someone you have hurt, may also help your situation.
Inadequacy	Get excited, review your perceptions and accept the message that you need to do something to get better, if it's a valid perception.
Overwhelmed/depressed	You need to re–evaluate your priorities and what's important to you. Make the list, prioritise and take action. The moment you deal with one thing you gain control and confidence and start to feel better.

Lonely	You need a connection with people — not just an intimate connection, it could be the friendship of someone to laugh with. Loneliness tells us we really want to be with people.

Reflecting on my language and emotions of late, I have noticed that there is a very close relationship between the emotions of anxiety and excitement and choosing the word excitement could offer me new and different opportunities! I have learnt that every emotion I have, is based on the interpretation I give to it and to change my emotions. I have to look at what meaning I'm giving to things and to try and find a better one.

I am now going to get into my hot tub with a clear head and a cup of coffee, focusing on the happiness of now. ☺ xx

15th February

Since my birthday celebrations ten days ago, when I didn't drink, I've found myself in a bit of a downward spiral.

I feel proud of myself that I didn't drink on my birthday, however, I can't say I fully enjoyed not drinking and for days I've been questioning myself again as to why I'm putting myself through this because the joy seems elusive. On a regular basis, I feel moments of joy, I feel okay and calm, but there are more occurrences than I would like of an underlying current of sadness.

I think the pandemic and lockdown now is hitting me in a way that it hasn't done before, which isn't helping...

I didn't cope well with Valentine's Day alone and looking at social media of everyone else's days. I know — why do I do it to myself?

I've done a lot of searching over the past 24 hours and I think I've worked out part of what is going on with me. The joy, pride and love in my life that I was feeling over the couple of weeks prior to my birthday, doesn't feel familiar and I've been mad busy with life.

I've got used to being kinder to myself, however, part of this has been telling myself it's okay to eat cake and takeaway on my birthday and not exercise. I've eaten 16,000 calories over my weekly intake in cupcakes and cake jars from my Goddaughter's cake shop – WTF!! ... Adam is going to shout a lot when I send my actual food intake for this week...Picture Adam, my fitness coach – he's the picture of health, on the front cover of Mens Health and I'm confessing to eating 16,000 calories in cake.

After chatting to Adam, for my check–in of what I've eaten and what exercise I've done in the week, I spend some time refocusing on my values. I realise there is a balance of freedom and discipline that aligns with the desires I have for my life. It's not going to happen by sitting on the sofa eating cake, as much as I would like that to be the case.

My goal this week is to get myself back into the good space I was in. I realise I need time on my own and to reconnect with myself, to learn, reflect, grow and move forwards. I need to find a new way to be in my life, with my life commitments and not be overwhelmed by duties and obligations.

I also know, that I need to prioritise my eight hours sleep. A non-negotiable which has, on more than one occasion recently, been compromised. I know this has impacted on my mental and physical health of late.

I am reading advice from various sleep experts who tell me to:

• Establish a routine: try to go to bed at the same time and wake up at the same time every day. Having a sleep routine will let your mind and body know that it's time to wind down. Get up and make your bed, no matter what.

• Relax before you go to bed: do something relaxing such as listening to music or having a bath. Also, relax your mind with things such as meditation, breathing exercises or visualisation. However, don't visualise something that excites you and keeps you awake! Visualise something calming that stills your mind.

• Make sure your bedroom is pleasant; that it's calming and the temperature, light and noise levels aid your sleep.

• Keep a note of your sleep patterns.

• If you have anything you are worried about, write it down and leave it in a notebook next to your bed.

• Give yourself a break from technology at least two hours before you go to bed; blue screens of phones and laptops have been shown to adversely affect sleep. Give your mind some preparation time.

• Take a look at your diet and exercise routine; caffeine, sugar and alcohol can all disturb sleep patterns. I know for me, if I drink coffee in the afternoon, it will affect my sleep that night.

28th February

In January I went back to I work and my energy levels started to return. However, so did the complexity and stress of daily life. I had previously been walking the dogs in the sunlight. Now I'm lucky if I'm walking them before 11pm, obviously totally disregarding the safety risks associated with this and dog theft, which my parents are very vocal and concerned about.

My inner child has been a little neglected over this period of time. Not only because of stress, but because some of my self– care rituals changed without me even realising it.

Since my separation, I was finding it a challenge to look after the dogs with everything else I was trying to do. Me, Hope and Kelsang found a new way of being whilst I was off with Covid and we learned to enjoy each other's company more. We would spend time together cuddling, chatting and walking – they were definitely part of my healing process. When I took Hope out first thing in the morning, I got into a habit of standing on the grass bare footed, feeling the earth under my feet, looking at the sky and taking in the weather.

Since I have gone back to work and Em has gone back to school, dog walking has become a chore again and I have done this in a rush with my shoes on, ready to take Em to school. Unbeknown to me, I lost my way of grounding and connecting with myself in the morning. It was only as I stood there, last Thursday, irritated and questioning why this wasn't as enjoyable as it used to be, I realised I was standing there with my shoes on and not feeling connected to anything. For the past few weeks, I've been feeling like I'm floating through every day, rather than being connected to the earth. I have reintroduced my barefoot ritual with Hope, I now feel so much more grounded again and connected as I start my day.

As I started to put my grounding ritual back in place (which wasn't actually one of my 5 non–negotiables – it is now), I realised that connecting to my inner child every day had also slipped off my list on many days. I felt that if I felt a moment of joy experiencing nature, feeling good about myself or looking at something of beauty (my fresh flowers in a vase are a weekly treat to myself) then that was enough. I realised it wasn't. I forgot that I needed to make time to play. I had forgotten my dancing, my singing and my rebounding. Slowly, I have started to put these things back in place and I am starting to feel more complete again! I have been doing online salsa lessons. One of the biggest things I am looking forward to is the salsa clubs reopening in Manchester, so that I can drive and have a fabulous night dancing, with no hangover the day after!

My 5 new 5 non–negotiables

1. Start my day positively: my gratitude diary, prayer and a daily bible reading to keep me connected with God.

2. 20 minutes of meditation and connecting with the grass.

3. Move for 30 minutes each day.

4. Connect to my inner child each day – I know she loves dancing, singing, baking, being outdoors on her terms (especially being in the sunshine and in water).

5. Write for 30 minutes every day (and achieve another bucket list item of mine in completing this book).

Other givens: 8 hours sleep, good nutrition, vitamins, water and being alcohol–free.

7th March

It's International Women's Day tomorrow and I have been invited to speak at an event this afternoon to share my story of Finding Joy Within. I've got to be honest with myself...I'm feeling nervous, as the organisers have told me it's a celebration event and I'm not feeling like my story is one full of celebration. It's full of ups and downs, twists and turns and not the perfect fairytale ending yet. That's life though, right? I debated changing my topic, to go with something safer and more positive. Then I thought that isn't me – go with who I am. I shared some of the things I have shared in this book and received some lovely feedback from people who had resonated with my journey. The experience gave me the confidence to finish writing this book, even though I am still a work in progress.

7th April

I've been very stuck in my head for the past week or so and have been doing some emotional eating. I was married on Easter Saturday, 23 years ago. We renewed our vows on Easter Sunday 15 years ago. Also, Em was Christened and Confirmed on Easter Sunday, so I have some quite significant happy family memories associated with the Easter period. I was not looking forward to my first Easter post–separation without alcohol. Last year I was distracted with the business of work, and I had alcohol as my crutch.

This weekend has been my first time socialising with people outside my support bubble, since Christmas, over the Easter weekend.

I had to work hard on my beliefs throughout the weekend about not drinking and not having fun. Very much the same as those that were arising for me at Christmas.

My belief; I will be miserable without alcohol. Others will be drinking. If I could drink, it would reduce my anxieties, help me feel more relaxed and help me to connect better with people. I love the taste and I'm craving that crisp taste of fizz at the back of my throat. My experience will be incomplete without alcohol.

My clarity; I am choosing not to drink for the following reasons...

• I want to be hangover and depression–free the day after.

• I don't want the impact of the calories from alcohol and what I might eat as a consequence.

• It's not enjoyable after the first one or two drinks, by then it has taken hold and I can't say no. The trade–offs of drinking aren't worth it.

• Not drinking is helping to build my confidence about making positive changes in my life. It is giving me a sense of confidence and achievement. I can drink if I want to, I am choosing not to.

• I miss what my body is telling me when I have had a drink.

• I want to experience true joy in my life without numbing pain or looking to a bottle for joy.

• I am role–modelling positive behaviour to Em.

• I am saving money on alcohol and taxis by not drinking.

• I can still be fun without alcohol.

• I can drink whatever and whenever I want any day. I am choosing it not to be today.

• I feel a little nervous and a bit excited and happy that I have chosen to be alcohol– free.

My new belief:

• I will be more present for people because I am focusing on them and not the bottle.

• I will do lovely fun things that I remember and have the freedom to leave if I am not enjoying myself.

• I won't be spending money on taxis. I will feel good about myself and know that every day and every new experience I am developing knowledge, skills and experience to help others and me lead more joyful and faith–filled lives.

Finding Joy Within™

• I have done this before at Christmas, and really enjoyed myself!

I went and had a lovely time at my three outdoor gatherings. I felt proud of myself when I was tucked up in bed with a cup of tea at midnight each night.

8th April

I watched Eat Pray Love this morning. I heard this quote, which resonated with me, at the end of the film which I love:

"In the end, I've come to believe in something I call "The Physics of the Quest."

A force in nature governed by laws as real as the laws of gravity.

The rule of Quest Physics goes something like this:

If you're brave enough to leave behind everything familiar and comforting,

which can be anything from your house to bitter, old resentments,

and set out on a truth–seeking journey, either externally or internally,

and if you are truly willing to regard everything that happens to you on that journey as a clue and if you accept everyone you meet along the way as a teacher

and if you are prepared, most of all, to face and forgive some very difficult realities about yourself,

then the truth will not be withheld from you."

– Liz Gilbert

I was inspired to go to Ingleton Waterfalls. It is somewhere I've always wanted to visit and I had some freedom today with a day off work and no plans. I had a lovely six mile walk and let go of some of the things I am still holding onto by burning a letter of my past hurts. (I am developing a quiet obsession with fire rituals ... ☺)

28th April

I've had a positive few weeks at work moving things forward with our integrated care agenda, however, I haven't determined what my new method of celebration is!

Now the world is opening back up again after Covid, I've done a few AF events over the past couple of weeks in the beer garden and BBQ's which have all been great and enjoyable, although it's not felt like the true celebration that I would've previously experienced when I popped a bottle cork! The best positive spin I've been able to put on any of these events is that I won't have a hangover in the morning, however, I've not felt the euphoria that others have had, which I've been slightly envious of.

Over the past couple of weeks I've tried walking, exercising, meditating, dancing, journaling in my brag book, reading, binge– watching 'The Bold Type' on Netflix, drinking coffee and relaxing in my hot tub to celebrate, all of which have all been absolutely lovely. Nothing however, has given me that high that alcohol did...

I will be 250 days AF on Monday, which I am so, so proud of and if you had told me this, this time last year, that I would've reached this point...I wouldn't have believed you! I do have a little voice in the back of my mind saying "F*** – what if I don't find another release button?" This is my next area of exploration and I'm taking comfort from Annie Grace that it took her a year or two to get to the joy feelings without alcohol.

23rd May

I am almost at the year mark since I started my alcohol quit journey. Last weekend I went to Simone's for afternoon tea with our friends for her birthday, which was lovely. I think it was about my twentieth social occasion AF in the last 12 months. Each time it gets easier. The amount of time I miss alcohol has reduced from all night to about thirty minutes. I don't feel like I'm missing out. The one thing I still crave is the taste, or so I thought.

Late in the evening, when it was dark outside, I accidentally picked up the wrong glass and sipped Prosecco. Whilst it tasted quite unpleasant, there was something immediately familiar and relaxing just from a sip, which I know is what my brain had got used to needing to survive. I know I need to continue with this process of trying to settle my stress system without alcohol and I made the right decision that moderation was not for me, as the immediate relaxation was a little frightening.

I am 270 days AF now. I was surprised at the familiarity and immediate calming effect from one sip, which reinforces that I couldn't just stop at one. At the time, I did think that no one would actually notice if I finished the glass, as they were all drinking. Here's the thing, I would know and for me, the risk of getting hooked again, is just too high.

30th May

It's one year today since I quit alcohol. I am back at the campsite in Pooley Bridge where, two years ago, I realised that my marriage was crumbling around me.

Finding Joy Within™

148

Two years ago, I was a broken mess not knowing how the hell I was going to survive. Today I am alcohol–free. I have created a new life for me and Em and I have started to love, accept and reconnect with myself, as I am. After going paddle boarding this morning with Leady and Jamie, on the beautiful Lake Ullswater where the fighter jets passed over us, I've cooked me and Em a bacon butty. I'm sat on the grass in front of my tent, sipping my cup of coffee and reflecting on the last 2 years of my life.

Prior to this holiday, I was anxious that coming back to the same place, with the same people, I would get caught in the trap of past memories, especially without the comfort of alcohol or treat food! Adam has been very clear with me that I need to stick as close as I can to my nutrition plan, as I have a photoshoot in seven weeks, so food as a distraction isn't an option for me either!

Before I came on this holiday, I spent some time visualising how I wanted to be, what I wanted to do and what I wanted to experience.

I want to:

• chill out!

• have fun with Em and my friends

• be alarm clock and tech–free for a week (other than taking photographs!)

• try new things from my bucket list

• nourish my body with good nutrition and movement to support the good work I've done over the past few weeks!

• enjoy being AF!

• reconnect with nature and spend time on my spiritual development

• go with the flow and forget time!

• listen to what my body is telling me it wants to do

• be filled with love, energy and gratitude for the life I am living. The past is behind me and the best is yet to come!

Having such clarity before this holiday has helped me to be positive about entering an environment that previously I had some negative associations with. I have had a beautiful holiday with Emma and my friends, done some fun things such as swimming, kayaking, paddle boarding and singing on the karaoke (much to the upset of our neighbours!) and have gained confidence in doing more things on my own.

I'm still an voyeger on this journey of finding my joy within and I know that until I can find happiness, without the help of a bottle, drinking is not for me. I'm not saying I will never drink again, for now though, I'm content on my journey of finding joy in the small and the big things.

My joy in the small things like looking after our dogs, looking after my plants, enjoying our home and even putting the bins out!

Also my joy in the big things like spending time with Emma, enjoying new experiences like paddle boarding, salsa dancing and late night driving experiences. Spending time with my incredible friends and most importantly, remembering all of the happy occasions from start to finish!

If I'm having a bad day, I set my joy alarm for every couple of hours to have a little dance! :-) If when I wake up and my vibration is low, I'll set my alarm for every couple of hours for one of my favourite songs to play and dance to 'Let's Get Loud' – an idea I borrowed from Preston Smiles! :-)

Two years after the separation, I am proud of the positive changes I have made to the way I live my life. I am actively nourishing my mind, body and spirit, learning to trust my gut instinct and relearning each day how to live without alcohol!

"You've got to make your own kind of music, sing your own special song, make your own kind of music, even if nobody else sings along."

- Cass Elliott

BEST DAY OF MY LIFE

Have you ever thought? I'll be happy when...

Fill in the dots for whatever it is for you. Whether it be a dream car, a new job, an exotic holiday, a partner, a bigger family or something much smaller. I can remember many days when getting home and opening a bottle of Prosecco had been my biggest fantasy of the day!

Have you ever had that situation happen, when something didn't quite feel like you thought it would, once it had happened? Or that the happiness was short lived?

The problem with many of the things above, is that they are mostly in the future or dependent on something external happening.

Now, don't get me wrong, I fully agree that things going on in your external world can heighten joy and happiness. My experience as a single mum during Covid has highlighted for me that there are definitely things I've missed that bring me an even greater sense of fun and joy. There are definitely things I took for granted, such as holidays, spending time with family and friends and days out to the beach. Not being able to do these things has made me appreciate and value how much more joy these things bring to my life.

However, through my journey I have also found that joy and happiness are states that are available to you every single day, irrespective of your circumstances, should you choose to look for them and be intentional about it. I believe you can cultivate your own joy and happiness right now in this moment, any moment, by focusing on the right things.

Through my research, study and experience, I have found there are five essential ingredients to living a joyful life, which I hope might be helpful to you on your quest for joy.

I have developed my uniquely designed framework, called The Joyful Life Liberator™, which includes what I believe are five of the crucial ingredients to living a life filled with joy and happiness.

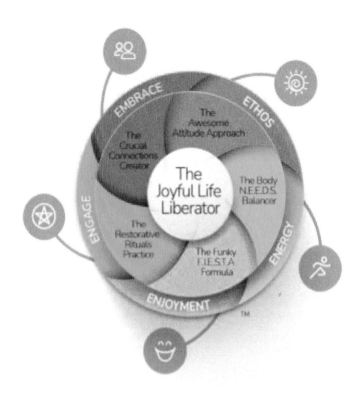

1. Embrace

So what do I mean by embrace? Well I mean embrace yourself. Connect with yourself, accept yourself and learn to love yourself. Not in an arrogant way, in a way that is underlining your brilliance as a human being!

Connecting with yourself and recognising what you are experiencing in your thoughts and emotions, is the key to mastering your life. If you can't connect with what you are experiencing and why, you can become susceptible to reacting to the behaviours of others. Prior to practicing mindfulness and meditation and being able to manage my thoughts and emotions, I was constantly reacting to others, because I didn't understand what was going on inside of me.

I believe that love and acceptance, for all parts of you, is key to being in happy and healthy relationships. If you don't love yourself (and all parts of yourself, including the bad ones!), how can you expect anyone else to?

Any difficulties in relationships are showing you that there is something that needs to grow inside of you, something that needs to heal internally or something that you need to see in yourself. Immediately after my separation, I struggled to be around happy couples, which most of my friends fortunately are. Not because I didn't want to be with the people, because I was jealous of their situation. Their happiness was highlighting something that I didn't have in my life, which I deeply desired. It took my negative emotions to discover this.

The relationship you have with yourself, is the most important relationship you will ever have. Knowing and accepting all parts of you, treating yourself with kindness and compassion, trusting your inner authority and valuing yourself, I believe is your route to joy. It isn't just how you embrace yourself that will determine

Finding Joy Within™

your happiness, it's how you embrace others too. Everybody is doing the best they can, with the resources they have. We will never understand how other people see things and their motives. Approaching everything you do with compassion and treating others with compassion, will leave you feeling good. You never know what anybody else is experiencing or what might have already happened in their day or life. It's important though to set boundaries and find a way to express your views in an empowering and kind way. If you do what others want you to do all of the time, you will lose yourself.

To be the best you can be, it's important that you have people in your life who uplift you. I am blessed in my life to have many of these! Jim Rohn famously said that you are the average of the five people you spend the most time with. There is an inherent truth that we, as social creatures, pick up on the habits, behaviours and attitudes of those around us. So this means that if you need to build the strength and positivity to get through anything, you need to keep your circle of friends and associates as healthy as you can.

2. Ethos

In western society, I don't think we adopt the ethos of living consciously widely enough. Many people are constantly on their phones, not listening properly to other people and ignoring the data their emotions are giving them. I think that Covid has given us a greater opportunity to slow down, tune in and notice things more. I still believe we need to be more mindful as a society and take time to notice small things, because one day, these will be the big things.

I also believe that as well as being mindful, mindset is also important. Some strategies for improving mindset include:

• Know how to change your emotional state; focusing on negativity constantly can take us to dark places, where it is not good to be. I'm not saying ignore negativity completely, because that can be bad for our well–being too. I believe we all need strategies to acknowledge our emotions and then shift our emotional state to a better, more positive place. At the start, it may take days to flip your mindset, with practice, these strategies will enable you to transform situations within a matter of minutes. Everybody's switch will be different, it's important you know what yours is. It might be exercise, watching Netflix, singing, craftwork, fishing, golf or something else?

• Believe in yourself and know that you can make changes in your life. Whatever challenge you are facing, willpower will only get you so far. Change your beliefs and watch the magic happen!

• Act as if and you will receive. Know what your ideal life, year, month, week and day look like and know that the universe has your back. Trust that the universe will deliver what you need, when you need it.

• Practice feeling true gratitude. You cannot feel grateful and unhappy at the same time.

Finding Joy Within™

• Start your day intentionally and try to stay away from technology at the start of the day. Visualise the great things that you can see happening in the day

• Start a Brag book and be proud of your accomplishments! Building pride in yourself will also build your confidence

• Live in the moment and let go of the little things. In 100 years, will it matter? The only thing we have is now.

3. Energy

We all know about the benefits of exercising and eating a healthy diet. However, without energy, it can be more difficult to build these things into your day. If you're waking up knackered, or in pain, prioritising exercise probably isn't going to seem too important. A sugary snack or a glass of wine may seem a much more attractive option than physical exercise.

Whether you are fit and healthy or suffering from any health issues, procrastination and overwhelm can easily become your best friend. So it's important that you know what it is you need to do to keep your body fit and strong and if you are suffering from any physical pain, that you know how you might be able to alleviate it. Only you know what the solutions are for you. Mindfully tune into your body and ask it everyday what it needs today.

Think about the battery in your mobile phone – if the amount of charge had gone to the RED zone – you'd be frantically looking round for a charger. We all need to be aware of when our bodies are in the red zone and know our own strategies to recharge our batteries. It's important to know that feeling when you're mentally, emotionally or spiritually depleted, as it can also impact on your physical health. So it's important to be able to connect with how you are, in all aspects of your life.

It's not just exercise and what we put in our bodies that can help our energy levels, it's also getting adequate sleep, enough downtime from technology and being in environments that lift our energetic vibrations.

Make your home somewhere that you love and want to be, that nourishes your soul. Put things that you love in every room that uplift you, whether that be colour, fresh flowers, artwork or something else and don't forget to get out into nature.

Studies looking at brain activity of people after three days of being in nature reveal lower levels of theta activity suggesting that their brains had rested. This is so important as our brain uses 20% of the oxygen and blood in our bodies.

As the great Jim Rohn said, "Look after your body. It's the only place that you ever have to live."

4. Enjoyment

I have experienced ridicule from some about prioritising my enjoyment intentionally and having fun as an adult. I truly believe that the purpose of life is to thrive and not just survive and having fun is so important for our health! If we don't enjoy ourselves, have fun and relax, our bodies become rigid, contract and we become more susceptible to ill health, so we need to have strategies to unwind, to laugh and to have fun!

If we are smiling, we are not only exercising our facial muscles, we are also likely to improve our mood and the mood of others around us too.

There are 5 reasons science suggests you should have more fun:

1. It improves relationships

2. It makes us smarter

3. It reduces stress

4. It balances hormones that lead to stress

5. It can make you more energetic and youthful

Laughter yoga is a real thing shown to have health and productivity benefits!

Barbara Frederickson (who I mentioned earlier) is well known for her work on the ten positive emotional states and demonstrating the positive impact they have on resilience, wellbeing and health. By doing things already described in the ingredients of embrace, ethos and energy, you will naturally experience some of the positive emotional states I have described below:

Joy: A moment when everything is exactly as it should be.

Gratitude: A moment when you realise how lucky you are, either because of a circumstance or because of something someone has done to help you.

Serenity: A state of relaxation or indulgence.

Interest: When something makes you curious.

Hope: You know that even in a difficult circumstance, that light will follow the darkness.

Pride: You're doing something you didn't think was possible or something that has taken you a lot of effort.

Amusement: The moments that you laugh and you have a new perspective on life.

Inspiration: Something that moves or motivates you to do something or be something different.

Awe: When you see brilliance in front of you. It might be a force of nature or something a person has achieved.

Love: You are likely to feel love interspersed with many of the above, in particular gratitude. Love is the thing that keeps us connected to each other.

As someone who isn't naturally a fun or playful person, I have to intentionally focus on creating amusement in my life and not just through reading or watching things that make me laugh (though they help), but by intentionally having fun in my life.

Creating my bucket list helped me to think of the fun things I wanted to do. However, each day, I also set myself a joy alarm, where I check in with my emotions. If I'm feeling negative or like something is missing, I'll do something to change my state. One of the advantages of me working from home is that I can pop and see the dogs for a couple of minutes. I can bounce on my rebounder and I also now have a swing in my back garden, which helps me to feel free after a couple of minutes!

The key to having fun, is through your inner child. It's important to talk to your inner child to keep them safe and secure. If you have had bad childhood experiences, it's important to make peace with them and teach your inner child that it's safe to enjoy themselves again. This won't necessarily be a quick process, however, opening the door to joy for your inner child, is such a crucial key to experiencing passion and fun in your life again. You may have experiences you can draw on from when you were young, to give you ideas of fun play activities to do. However, if you are anything like me, you might be starting with a blank sheet of paper of things you've always wanted to experience and that offers up a whole range of new opportunities! For me, it was sports activities, singing, dancing and writing.

To genuinely experience joy every day, I believe it's about noticing the joyful moments that happen daily, without any need for creation and also intentionally doing the things that bring more of the positive emotional states into your life.

5. Engage

The rituals by which we live our lives, are another path to our joy. I believe if you don't put rituals into place and you don't consciously prioritise your mental, physical, emotional and spiritual wellbeing, you will continue to experience struggles in your life. I think many of us know what we need to do to be become happier. However, here's the thing, we read and don't take action. We plan to start tomorrow. I have certainly been there with my years of shelf–development, rather than self–development. I think I have more shelf-help books than my local library!

To experience more joy today, it's likely that you will need to make some changes to your day. For each one of us, the focus needed for each ingredient will be very different. For example, I find it easy to meditate and drink water. I used to find it quite an effort to get out of the house and exercise and say no to that cake or glass of wine that I knew would make me feel bad afterwards. You will know your own hotspots and the plans you need to put in place to manage them. This will need constant adjustment in different seasons of your life.

You will notice that, as you start to make a change in one part of your life, you will see dramatic impacts in other dimensions of your world and very quickly too. This is known as the compound effect. For me, addressing my alcohol consumption, positively impacted in every other aspect of my life – my desire to be outdoors, to nourish my body with things that are good for me, to connect with my inner child and to have fun!

Trust me, when I say you are able to make significant changes in your life, in relatively short periods of time. If you have a vision for your life and you take hourly, daily, weekly, monthly and yearly action to move towards it you will start to notice shifts. Many authors have written about how to change habits.

James Clear and Charles Duhigg both describe powerful ways to build new habits and break old ones. However, it takes courage. It means stepping out of your old habits and embracing new ones.

As you know, I've had so many attempts at establishing rituals that are constantly evolving, relating to the season of my life that I am in. If things aren't working for me, I don't see them as failure anymore or give myself a hard time. I see this as learning and make some changes.

Learning comes at edge of uncertainty and as Joseph Campbell says, "The cave you fear to enter holds the treasure you seek."

"You have to fight through some bad days to earn the best days of your life."

- Adnan

YOU ARE THE REASON

I believe we are all here to make a difference and contribute throughout our lives.

If we live our lives consciously, passionately, joyfully, and intentionally, we will not only change our world, but the world of others around us too.

Every day we wake up, we have been blessed with a new opportunity. Another 1440 minutes to live the life we want to live and we are not guaranteed tomorrow. If there is anything this pandemic has taught me, it's about how young, fit, healthy people, as well as more vulnerable elderly people are sadly being taken too early from this world.

Some people might believe, as I once did, that happiness isn't for them, it's just for special people, but it's not. Happiness is for all of us. God created us all to live joyful lives, not just some of us, all of us.

This book has been forty–four years in the making and three years in the writing. Until I began experiencing love, peace, acceptance and joy, I didn't feel authentic enough to share my story. There were challenges I had to endure, hurdles I had to overcome and rituals for me to embed, before I could write this book truly from the heart. I am not perfect, I still make mistakes and I am still learning many new skills in my life, especially in my sobriety. However, I believe I have enough knowledge to share, that might just help one person live a more joyful life.

The Starfish Story by Loren Eiseley is one of my favourite stories and resonates with me as to why I have written this book.

Once upon a time, there was an old man who used to go to the ocean to do his writing. He had a habit of walking on the beach every morning before he began his work.

Finding Joy Within™

Early one morning, he was walking along the shore after a big storm had passed and found the vast beach littered with starfish as far as the eye could see, stretching in both directions. Off in the distance, the old man noticed a small boy approaching.

As the boy walked, he paused every so often and as he grew closer, the man could see that he was occasionally bending down to pick up an object and throw it into the sea.

The boy came closer still and the man called out, "Good morning! May I ask what it is that you are doing?"

The young boy paused, looked up, and replied, "Throwing starfish back into the ocean. The tide has washed them up onto the beach and they can't return to the sea by themselves," the youth replied. "When the sun gets high, they will die, unless I throw them back into the water."

The old man replied, "But there must be tens of thousands of starfish on this beach. I'm afraid you won't really be able to make much of a difference."

The boy bent down, picked up yet another starfish and threw it as far as he could into the ocean. Then he turned, smiled and said, "It made a difference to that one!"

I know the feeling, I am looking for when I am in flow and connected to my soul's purpose. I call it my heart–centred pride feeling. It's a colourful vibration that fills my whole body. When I am being a good mum to Emma, doing something positive in my leadership role, doing something good for myself or others, or moving towards the vision I have for my life, I know I am on the right path because I have that warm feeling inside of me and my life feels colourful. For many years I didn't have this, hence why I couldn't write this book.

I know that life will always continue to throw me challenges and I know that whatever I am faced with I can overcome because:

• I am enough.

• I am loved by God and those around me.

• I know that I am blessed with the best daughter, friends and family that a woman could wish for.

• If it's not okay, it's not the end. There is still something the universe is trying to teach me.

• Creating my joy is in my gift. There are bursts of happiness to be found in every single day and in every single moment, if I take time to find and appreciate them.

Over the last twelve months, I have discovered that being a woman is not about being at WAR with yourself or others. I believe it's about being RAW. It's about being Real, Authentic and Wise. It's about showing up as you and always trusting your intuition to guide you on the right path.

I am now truly grateful for all the challenges I have faced in my life, as they have enabled me to fully get to know me, to understand my values and dream about my future.

I am truly grateful to the Universe for:

• Emma and my beautiful relationship with her.

• My parents who love and support me.

• My friends who love and support me.

• Glen for giving me Emma, some wonderful memories and another chance for us to be happy in a different way.

• My beautiful dogs, who always look at me with love in their eyes (especially when I give them cheese ☺).

• My lovely home and my beautiful garden.

• My health.

• The professional and personal development support I have received over the years.

• The talents and gifts that God has given me to enable me to pursue my career.

• Lovely experiences and holidays I've had throughout my life.

• New opportunities in my life.

• Covid – it forced me to value my health, to stop and grieve, to practise patience and rebuild my life on spirituality. I know that I need to prioritise meditation and movement and to look after my energy, to smile, be present and optimistic.

• My life with Emma

And I am immensely proud of:

• Emma and the lovely times we have together

• My focus and determination

• The fact I have worked hard on myself, re–patterning my beliefs, finding new ways of being and having a different outlook on life

• My friendships

• Prioritising my heath and building in good nutrition and movement most days

• My career, my qualifications and establishing my own business

• Managing to navigate a divorce process

• My beautiful home and garden

• Coming to a place of acceptance and forgiveness of things that have happened in my life

• Getting better at managing my money

• My sporting achievements – a marathon, 3 triathlons and a virtual 50 mile race over 4 days

• Being able to do some practical stuff around the house – I built my bed, I know how to change a light bulb and I can configure my Sonos speaker (small steps...)

• Managing the house tasks on my own every week – Emma always has food and clean clothes!

• Life is okay, in fact, more than okay, on my own

• I am 280 days alcohol–free and it has been one whole year today since I started my sobriety journey! I never thought this would have been possible. I remember looking at the One Year No Beer literature on so many occasions thinking how on earth do people do that!

• I have written this book ☺

Twelve months ago I couldn't have written a list that I was proud of – it would have felt way too egotistical! Now, I know it's important for my mental health to remember something I'm proud of each day.

I started my journey of personal development when I was in my twenties and it's taken me years to learn the things I needed to put in place to make me smile every day. I know that darkness is a place I could very easily find myself in again if I am not intentional about how I live my life every single day. That might seem like hard work to some and occasionally it is. I truly believe that joy lies on the other side of intentionality.

Finding Joy Within™

I am still a work in progress and I don't have all the answers, I hope that this book may give you some comfort or inspiration, especially if you are facing challenges in your life, to intentionally find more joy and pleasure in your life by looking within.

Always keep in your heart one of life's famous quotes, "The greater the storm the brighter the rainbow."

Much love, Kath xx

"I believe I'm here for a reason and my purpose is greater than my challenges!"

- **Dawn Nocera**

BOOKS I RECOMMEND

A Better Way to Think: By Norman Wright

Atomic Habits: By James Clear

Awaken The Giant Within: By Anthony Robbins

Chicken Soup For The Soul: By Jack Canfield and Mark Victor Hansen

Feel The Fear and Do It Anyway: By Susan Jeffers

Find Your Why: By Cheryl Chapman and Marion Bevington

Flow: The Psychology of optimal experience. By Mihaly Csikszentmihalyi

Focusing: By Eugene Gendlin

Habits of a Godly Woman: By Joyce Meyer

Keys To Unlocking Your Back Pain: By Sophia Kupse

Living A Life You Love: By Joyce Meyer

Love Louder: By Preston Smiles

Mindfulness: A Practical Guide to Finding Peace in a Frantic World: By Mark Williams and Dr Danny Penman

Mrs D Is Going Without: By Lotta Dann

Real Happiness: By Sharon Salzberg

The Alchemist: Paul Coelho

The Book Of Forgiving: By Desmond &Mpho Tutu

The Breakthrough Experience: Dr John F. Demartini

The Chimp Paradox: By Steve Peters

The Compound Effect: By Darren Hardy

The Miracle Morning: By Hal Elrod

The Monk Who Sold His Ferrari: By Robin Sharma

The Power Of Habit: By Charles Duhigg

The Secret: By Rhonda Byrne

The 28 Day Alcohol Free Challenge: By Andy Ramage

This Naked Mind: By Annie Grace

Super Attractor: By Gabrielle Berstein

Unleash The Power Within: By Anthony Robbins

We Are The Luckiest: By Laura McKowen

Your Best Year Yet: By Jenny Ditzler

RESEARCH FEATURED WITHIN THIS BOOK

Chiesa A1, Serretti A. Mindfulness–based stress reduction for stress management in healthy people: a review and meta–analysis. J Altern Complement Med. 2009 May;15(5):593–600.

Fredrickson, Barbara L.; Cohn, Michael A.; Coffey, Kimberly A.; Pek, Jolynn; Finkel, Sandra M. Open hearts build lives: Positive emotions, induced through loving–kindness meditation, build consequential personal resources. Journal of Personality and Social Psychology, Vol 95(5), Nov 2008, 1045–1062.

Grewen, K. M., Anderson, B. J., Girdler, S. S., Light, K. C. (2003). Warm partner contact is related to lower cardiovascular reactivity. Behavioral Medicine, 29, 123–130.

https://www.healthline.com/health/hugging–benefits: The benefits of hugs

Hidenobu Sumioka, Aya Nakae, Ryota Kanai and Hiroshi Ishiguro (2013). Huggable communication medium decreases cortisol levels. Sci Rep. 2013; 3: 3034.

Lieberman M, et al. Putting feelings into words: Affect labelling disrupts Amygdala Activity in Response to Affective Stimuli. Psychological Science 2007;18(5):421–428.

Lieberman M, et al. Subjective Responses to Emotional Stimuli During Labeling, Reappraisal, and Distraction. Emotion 2011;11(3):468–480.

Lyubomirsky S, et al. The Benefits of Frequent Positive Affect: Does Happiness Lead to Success? Psychological Bulletin (Nov. 2005): Vol. 131, No. 6, pp. 803–55.

Luders E, Cherbuin N, Kurth F (2015). Forever Young(er): potential age–defying effects of long–term meditation on gray matter atrophy. Frontiers in Psychology. 5: 1551.

Murphy MLM, Janicki–Deverts D, Cohen S (2018) Receiving a hug is associated with the attenuation of negative mood that occurs on days with interpersonal conflict. PLOS ONE 13(10).

Nakata H, Sakamoto K, Kakigi R (2014). Meditation reduces pain–related neural activity in the anterior cingulate cortex, insula, secondary somatosensory cortex, and thalamus Frontiers in Psychology. 5:1489.

http://positivepsychology.org.uk/what–is–positive–psychology/: The evidence on gratitude

https://www.rcpsych.ac.uk/mental–health/treatments–and–wellbeing/cognitive–behavioural–therapy–(cbt)

https://tlexinstitute.com/how-to-effortlessly-have-more-positive-thoughts/

Schneider, R et al. Stress Reduction in the Secondary Prevention of Cardiovascular Disease: Randomized, Controlled Trial of Transcendental Meditation and Health Education in Blacks. Circ Cardiovasc Qual Outcomes, November 13 2012

Seligman ME, et al. Positive Psychology: An Introduction, American Psychologist (Jan. 2000): Vol. 55, No. 1, pp. 5–14.

Seligman ME, et al. Positive Psychology Progress: Empirical Validation of Interventions, American Psychologist (July–Aug. 2005): Vol. 60, No. 5, pp. 410–21.

Sharma M, Rush SE (October 2014). Mindfulness–based stress reduction as a stress management intervention for healthy individuals: a systematic review. Journal of Evidence–Based Complementary & Alternative Medicine. 19(4): 271–86.

Siegel, D.J. (2009). Mindful awareness, mindsight, and neural integration. The Humanistic Psychologist, 37(2), 137–158.

Siegel, D.J. (2007). Mindfulness training and neural integration. Journal of Social, Cognitive, and Affective Neuroscience, 2(4), 259– 263.

Siegel, D.J. (2007). The mindful brain: Reflection and attunement in the cultivation of well–being. New York: W.W. Norton & Company.

FINDING OUT MORE

I would like to thank you for reading this book

If you are interested in learning more about the tools, strategies and approaches I have described in this book, please visit my website:

www.workwithkath.co.uk

Or you can follow me on your preferred social media by checking out my:

www.linktr.ee/TheJoyExplorer

ACKNOWLEDGEMENTS

I am truly grateful for all the help, support and inspiration I have had through my life from many different places. Without the love, kindness and influence of many different people in my life, I wouldn't be the person I am today.

I am grateful to Emma for the inspiration she gives me every day to be a better person.

I am grateful to my Mum and Dad for loving me and always doing what they can to support me.

I am grateful to my Grandparents and Godparents for the support they gave me when I was younger.

I am grateful to all my family and friends for the love and support they have given, especially over the past 2 years, which have been the most challenging of my life. In particular:

Vicky, Ellie and Jack, Claire, Ian, Zoe and Anna, Andre and Simone, Andy, Vicki and Phoebe, Natalie, Clive, Sebastian and Mia, Mel, Mark and Brooke, Rosie, Jamie and Juliette

I am grateful to Sue, Matt, Harry and Lottie for all the help they gladly give to help me look after the dogs.

I am grateful to Glen for the happy times we had together and for our daughter Emma.

I am grateful to Liz for her friendship and spiritual guidance.

I am grateful to my colleagues in Bury who have supported me personally and professionally in my journey.

I am grateful to Michelle Watson for persevering with me until the time was right to publish this book.

Finding Joy Within™

I am grateful to Jodie Lee Liggett for her beautiful artwork on the book cover.

I am grateful to those who have helped me directly in the personal development, business development and therapeutic world. In particular Cheryl Chapman, Sophia Kupse, Adele Marie Hartshorn, Marion Bevington, Andy Harrington, Janine Dunn, Adam Bates, Suzanne Roynon, Michelle Coops, Annie Grace, Lisa King, Emma Sneddon and Steve Taylor.

I am grateful for the support I have had from the communities I belong to including Ab–Fit, Clarity, Focus and Growth, the Live Love Laugh Lounge, the Naked Mind Community and the Professional Speakers Academy.

I am grateful to all those who have shared their sobriety and personal development journeys online and in their books, which have inspired me throughout over the past 20 years.

I am grateful for the support I have found within me, from God and the Universe to write this book.

Finding Joy Within™

ABOUT THE AUTHOR

Finding Joy Within™

Kath is a Mum, who is passionate about helping people live their lives with joy, purpose and authenticity.

She is a TEDx speaker, motivated to share the struggles of how painful it can be to remove distractions from your life and equally how joyful taking the journey to intentionally can be!

She is an experienced Health and Care Sector Director and is passionate about the sustainability of public services, especially with the challenges facing our population and our health and care workforce following the Pandemic.

As an experienced Executive Coach and Meditation Teacher, Kath is passionate about inspiring people to live joyful lives, not only to help themselves, but to also help to build thriving families and communities.

Kath is passionate about creating environments that enable people to take responsibility for their own self-love and self-care with compassion.

"I believe if you face into your fears, the messiness and the darkness, you can find your wisdom, joy and light"

- Kath Wynne-Jones

AUTHOR CREDENTIALS

B.Sc (Hons) Medical Informatics : Manchester University

Master of Philosophy: Manchester University

PG Cert in Executive Coaching: Leeds Beckett University

PG Diploma in Psychology: Leeds Beckett University

EMCC Senior Practitioner Level Coaching Programme: European Mentoring and Coaching Programme

NHS leadership academy award in Executive Healthcare Leadership: NHS Leadership Academy

Diploma in Meditation Teaching: British School of Meditation

AQUA Integrated Care Research Fellow

TEDX Speaker

ACE Mentor for The Professional Speakers Academy

Currently studying towards Level 4 Nutrition Coaching

Finding Joy Within™

THOUGHTS ABOUT THE AUTHOR AND BOOK

There is a quote by Susan Gale that states … Sometimes quiet people really do have a lot to say. They're just being careful who they open up to.

I'd love to say that I can remember the first time I met Kath, in full detail and yet the truth is I don't. That could be for many reasons. As a speaker who stands on stage in front of hundreds of people and an integral part of The Professional Speakers Academy, I meet a lot of people and whilst I'm good with faces, I'm not so good with names! My sense however is that it was because Kath wasn't one of those "look at me" significance seekers and so she quietly blended in.

What I do recall is her bright white smile, long dark hair, a fit looking body and a genuine sense of care for others. As a member of the A.C.E (Academy Coaching Executives), a group of people I mentor for Andy Harrington (you've heard about him before) Kath was the one laughing with the team, supporting them and using her skills from her leadership role. Her northern openness was welcomed by all.

When Kath applied to join The Find Your WHY Foundation I knew there was something she was searching for (clearly a purpose and to know who she was), little did we know how much the mantra of the Foundation "you don't have to figure it out on your own and you don't have to do it alone" would be crucial for her as she entered a period of change. I've seen Kath in her low times and at the same time I've witnessed her transition into the amazing being she really is.

I've seen the self–doubt and witnessed the moments of self–pride and I am truly grateful that she allowed myself and co–creator Marion Bevington to support her to Find her WHY and to provide platforms so she can be seen, be heard and be herself.

I'm a fan of her resilience and creativity and watching her create "The Joyful Life Liberator™" Program to help others, showing how leaders and managers in the development space can also experience joy in their life too, has been a pleasure.

The truth is no–one follows an unscarred general into battle and in this book, Kath shares honestly and from the heart, as an inspiration to anyone who is ready to peel back the façade of "I'm ok" and find a tangible way to develop themselves, to become even more incredible.

Recognise the gift Kath provides here as she opens up, warts and all, so that you can benefit from this WHY's woman too.

With love Cheryl Chapman

Cheryl Chapman - Visionary at The Find Your WHY Foundation and Creator of The Live Love Laugh Lives, helping you to Be Seen, Be Heard and Be YOU!

As a fellow traveler on the road where work dictated the speed, I was traveling at for the whole of my life, and I was using distractions as a substitute for true happiness, Kath's reflections resonate with my lived experience. I suspect that they will resonate with the experience of many.

There was a moment in my life when I was asked a question "You have a mission for your organisation, but do you have a mission for your life?". The answer was no. I was expert at developing and articulating purpose and direction for organisations, yet I had not thought to use the same skills and rigour when thinking about my happiness and that of those that are dear to me. It seems obvious now that I should have put the same energy into happiness as I did for work, but I didn't. I think prompts are needed to do so. Kath's reflections and insights are fascinating.

Here is a person that is like many in leadership positions. I have known her for many years. She never signaled or displayed signs of her inner turmoil. She is always a go to person. You know the job will be done, and done well, if Kath does it. Again, this is like so many of us. But what is the cost, if we don't truly know what gives us joy and act on it?

Being seen as being successful at work is not enough if you aren't really happy. Love and happiness are central to living a fulfilling life. Knowing that you can change the road you are on, knowing that you can steer a different course is what this book will challenge you to think of.

It's more than one woman's story. It is a story of the many in today's times. The global pandemic has caused many to re-evaluate what we want out of our time on earth. Kath's journey gives us hope and a way of thinking through what we could do to achieve happiness and joy.

Raj Jain – Former Chief Executive Officer, The Northern Care Alliance

From the moment I heard Kath speak at the 'Find Your Why' Annual Awards ceremony, early March 2020, I knew she was someone incredibly special. I automatically connected with her story, as did everyone in the audience, who had battled with some form of demon in their life. We both had similar high–profile backgrounds in leadership and development, but it was Kath's heartfelt and honest account of her recovery, from a broken marriage and struggle with distractions, that made her so credible, not only reducing me to tears, but also the rest of the listeners in the room.

My tears were not because I was listening to a victim, but because I was hearing the story of a champion, a young woman who had conquered her demons to inspire others. Kath's natural bubbly persona makes her the loveable lady she is, her joyful smile is infectious just like her laughter. You can't help, but immediately fall in love with Kath's zest for life and feel comfortable in her presence.

However, like most people, behind her positive veil, she carried her own life wounds. What makes this book so authentic is that Kath has lived through many challenges that most professional leaders can immediately connect with, masking their work and life pressures with a cheeky glass of red, falling silently into distraction and denial.

As an established author myself of three bestselling self–help books and 'Inner Child Back Pain Psychology' specialist, after working with Kath, I encouraged her to write this book to help and inspire others who may be facing the same battles behind a professional role. As each chapter unfolds, in this easy to read 'Dear Diary' style book, you share Kath's rollercoaster journey as she is challenged daily by the pressures of a leadership role and alcohol, acceptance of a lost marriage and how her inner child questions her need for sobriety.

Finding Joy Within™

Along the way, the reader learns and grows through Kath's remarkable story, on how to triumph over everyday life challenges, including alcohol. She writes from the heart with passion and purpose, delivering solutions grown from her own failures to demonstrate to the reader that recovery from anything is possible. When you go through the biggest challenges the best changes happen.

If you are now ready to ditch the alcohol or make the change from whatever distraction is causing you emotional pain that stops you from moving forward, this book is a must.

You will gain access to knowledge and understanding on how to make the change, with deep spiritual insights to succeed, slaying your dragon using Kath's no nonsense healing approach. The recommendations she offers, based on many years as a professional leader and coach, will allow you to engage in a more professional and personal balanced life 'Finding Joy Within.'

Finally, I feel not only blessed to know Kath, but also, honoured, humble and grateful to have been part of her healing journey. I am excited for you, the reader. You are about to venture into a wonderful new beginning.

Sophia Kupse - MSc Author, Innovator & Inner Child/ Back Pain Psychology Specialist Senior member of The Royal Society of Medicine

Printed in Great Britain
by Amazon

79533819R00108